The SEX EDcyclopedia

A COMPREHENSIVE GUIDE TO HEALTHY SEXUALITY, FOR THE MODERN, MALE TEEN.

Everything a guy needs to know, whether he is
sexually active or going to be someday...

Second Edition

Jo Langford, M.A.

ISBN: 978-1-61098-303-7
Ebook: 978-1-61098-304-4

Published by

The Nazca Plains Corporation ®
4640 Paradise Rd, Suite 141
Las Vegas, NV 89109-8000
© 2011 by The Nazca Plains Corporation. All rights reserved.

Cover Photo, Blake Stephens

Art Direction, Blake Stephens

The SEX EDcyclopedia

A COMPREHENSIVE GUIDE TO HEALTHY SEXUALITY, FOR THE MODERN, MALE TEEN.

Everything a guy needs to know, whether he is
sexually active or going to be someday...

Second Edition

Published by The Nazca Plains Corporation
Las Vegas, Nevada
2011

Acknowledgements

For my three most-importants: Amber, Xander and Bella. You three have taught me what it means to be strong, self-aware, and as much myself as I can be. I am hoping this book will allow me to pass some of that along to others. I am indebted to the three of you in more ways than I have words. Thank you for your support, your patience and your palpable, palpable love.

Thanks, also, to everyone who has helped me on this path, especially Ellen, Nick, Marilyn, Peter, Bill, Barbara, my boys; Mikey, Gregor and Gar', The Scooby Gang in general, Nick, Julia and Erik for their feedback, Richard Wagner and Seaton Gras for their time and Kristin Kildall for her gorgeous work on my logo.

Additional thanks are in order for

>Allena Gabosch for the fire under my butt, the connections and the editing.

>Amy Lang for the teamwork and ideas.

>Tim Kahn and Carol Almero for making space for me under their wings.

Dan Savage and Kidder Kaper, Gay Rick and Laura Rad have all been huge inspirations as well.

Thank you all,
Jo

Table of Contents

SECTION II – IDENTITY

PART THREE: THE OTHER INS and OUTS
SECTION III – RELATIONSHIPS

SECTION IV – SEXUAL ACTIVITY

SECTION V – CHOICE MAKING/ DECISION MAKING

PART FOUR: RISK REDUCTION
SECTION VI – RISK REDUCTION

SECTION VII – SEXUAL HEALTH

SECTION VIII – SEXUAL HARM

SECTION X – FOR PARENTS

PART FIVE: OUTRO

PART ONE: INTRO

Introduction

Whether you are waiting to be sexually active until marriage, until college or until this weekend, let this book help you protect yourselves from unintended pregnancy and sexually transmitted infection when you become sexually active.

If you are a teenage guy and holding this book in your hands:

- Statistically, somewhere around 300,000 of you guys are going to get someone pregnant before you graduate high school.[1]

- Approximately half of you are already sexually active in some way.[2]

- A quarter of those guys of have already gotten an STI.[3]

- A third of you have received an aggressive online solicitation from an online predator in the last year.[4]

- One out of every five of you has sent a picture of your penis to someone over telephone lines.[5]

Your parents have spent a great deal of time being worried about sexual predators during your lifetime-it's on the front page of every paper, websites and news channels are loaded with messages and warnings, but most of the sexual damage being done to you guys is being done to each other and yourselves.

The good news is this is preventable.

You all know about Defensive Driving Courses. The American National Standard Safe Practices for Motor Vehicle Operation defines Defensive Driving as "Driving to save lives, time and money, in spite of the conditions around you and the actions of others."[6]

Teenagers having sex doesn't scare me the way it scares some of your parents – Teenagers have been having sex since the beginning of time.

Actually, that is not completely true – teenagers having sex scares me in the same way teenagers driving scares me.

But as an adult (and a parent) (and a guy), I am a lot less worried when I know a particular person has:

- learned how to drive properly

- and drive safely

- and that they have made an effort to not have their driving impact their life (or the lives of the people around them) in a negative or adverse, life-changing way.

My goal is for this book to serve as a "Defensive Sexuality Course," of sorts.

It will provide skills and information for you to make informed decisions and give you the necessary tools to go at sex and sexuality with a sense of confidence and seriousness, having fun along the way, while doing as little harm to yourselves and each other as possible.

Loving and relating, "to save lives, time and money, in spite of the conditions around you and the actions of others."

A SPECIAL NOTE ABOUT THE VALUES
ASSOCIATED WITH THIS BOOK

- Appreciation of the difficulty and confusion associated with puberty and adolescence.

- Teens ought to be treated with respect.

- Young people should be encouraged and expected to be responsible for their own learning and experience, their own actions and reactions.

- Access to comprehensive sex education is every person's right.

- Providing comprehensive sex education is an adult responsibility.

- Vague terminology, sheepishness and avoidance around sex do not help anyone.

- Fear and ignorance around sexuality cause problems.

- All sex orientations and identities need to be acknowledged.

- The realities of teen sexual behavior and risk need to be acknowledged.

- Sex positive approaches and openness are the best ones – acknowledging the pleasure and health aspects of sex as well as the dangers and risks.

PART TWO: THE INS AND OUTS

SECTION I – BIOLOGY

Sexual health and mature sexual choices and behavior are both very much dependent on having a good understanding of both your own, and your partner's body.

Some parts are reproductive.

Some are sexual.

Some are both.

Chapter 1

THE GIRL PARTS

The female reproductive and sexual body parts are collectively known as the vulva – the parts you can see.

The **Vagina** is the part that most guys are excited about. It is also called the birth canal. The Vagina is very different from the penis in several ways, some of which are obvious and some of which are not. For example, some guys don't understand there is more than one opening down there.

The vagina is near (but is different than) the urethra, which is where urine leaves the body.

The vagina passes blood and substance during a girl's period, produces fluids which cleanse and lubricates itself and allows a pathway for sperm to reach the cervix (to cause pregnancy) and for the baby to leave the uterus (during birth)."

Vaginas are also commonly called "Gynes" (pronounced "Jines") or sometimes "pussies," (plus numerous other terms, but lets strive to use the big boy words).

The **cervix** is a small, doughnut-shaped organ, which connects the uterus and the back of the vagina.

The **hymen** is a thin, piece of tissue that sometimes can partially cover the opening of the vagina. This tissue often becomes broken at some point in a girl's life, though not always. Some people consider the presence of a hymen to mean virginity, though some woman are born without hymens, some have hymens that are never truly broken and many others have their hymens broken in ways other than sex.

The **mons** is the fatty tissue above a woman's pubic bone – the part usually covered with hair. This provides protection for the pubic bone during intercourse.

Two layers of lips or **labia**, majora (outer) and minora (inner) cover and protect the vagina, (and above that) the urethra and (above that) the clitoris.

The **clitoris** is a short shaft with a very sensitive tip, sometimes covered with a fold of skin (the clitoral hood). The clitoris is the only female organ whose sole purpose is pleasure, and it plays an incredibly important part of arousal for women. It is located at the top of the opening of the vagina, above the urethra.

The **ovaries** are ovum (or egg) producing, reproductive organs. Eggs contain the female DNA and twenty-three chromosomes, which (if joined by the DNA and chromosomes of a sperm) create an embryo.

Fallopian tubes (also known as oviducts) are about seven to fourteen centimeter long tubes, which lead the egg from the ovaries into the uterus after ovulation (the release of the egg). This is where eggs are fertilized.

The **Uterus** (or womb) is where the embryo attaches and eventually grows into a fetus during gestation.

The **Gräfenberg Spot**, or "G-Spot", is a female erogenous zone located inside the vagina. Erogenous zones are areas which, when stimulated, can lead to high levels of sexual arousal and powerful orgasms. The G-Spot is typically found on the inner front wall of the vagina (behind the pubic bone).

The **breasts** of a female body contain the mammary glands, which make milk used to feed infants. Nipples of female breasts are sensitive to touch and can enhance sexual pleasure. They also serve as a way for babies to access breast milk – though they can be loads of fun for the big boys as well.

Chapter 2

THE BOY PARTS

The penis is the main reproductive organ for male animals. It is also the one that we are most excited about. Penises also serve as a male method of urination. Penises are also commonly called "dicks" or sometimes "cocks," (plus numerous other terms, but lets strive to use the big boy words).

The **scrotum** is the sac of skin and muscle, which contains and (theoretically) protects the testicles. It is located between the penis and the anus.

Testicles (testes or "balls") are comprised of approximately 850 feet of tubules, which produce the male hormone, (testosterone) and make sperm. Like penises, balls come in all different shapes and sizes. Like penises, size, shape and texture vary as well. Fact: In over 80% of guys, the left one hangs a bit lower than the right.

Sperm are the male reproductive cells, comprised of twenty-three chromosomes. Sperm are stored in the epydidymis – the spongy layer of tubes located near the top of each testicle – where the sperm grow and mature.

The **foreskin** is a retractable, double-layered, fold of skin that covers and protects the glans of the penis when it is not erect. When a male is aroused, and his penis becomes erect (hard), the foreskin slips back to expose the glans. The **glans** is the sensitive "head" of the penis.

When the penis head is stimulated and the penis gets hard (an erection), the **vas deferens** transports sperm to the urethra. The urethra passes through the penis and opens to the outside to pass semen during ejaculation. This is where urine leaves the body as well.

Along the way, several other glands work to add secretions to the sperm as it through the body. Sperm and these other substances make up semen. **Semen** is a m. substance, which helps sperm travel safely out of the penis to its next destination, which is (sometimes) joining its DNA and chromosomes with that of a female egg to form an embryo.

The **prostate** gland is one of the glands that help create seminal fluid. The prostate is also called the "male G-Spot." The prostate gland is typically found a couple of inches inside the anus and forward along the front wall of the rectum (toward the belly button).

Stimulation of the prostate gland, through massage (with fingers) or anal intercourse (by a penis) can add sexual pleasure that is very different than the feelings caused when the head of the penis is stimulated.

The **anus** is the opening of the rectum, which is also highly sensitive to touch and can provide sexual pleasure.

Chapter 3

PUBERTY

Is the process, which begins adolescence – the transition between childhood and adulthood.

Both the male and female body will take on a different shape, and each will develop stronger sexual characteristics. New thoughts and feelings occur as the body changes at a rapid pace.

Physical, emotional and hormonal changes overlap. These changes do not occur on a strict timeline, which is one of the things that can make this time period difficult. The entire process can take anywhere from one to six years.

Puberty in females usually happens between the ages of eight and thirteen.

Male puberty usually occurs between nine to fourteen years of age.[7]

When the body is nearing sexual maturity, the brain releases chemicals called hormones. These are responsible for all of these changes. Hormones stimulate the ovaries of girls to produce hormones called estrogen and progesterone, and the testes of boys produce testosterone.

Growth hormones are also stimulated and make the body grow larger. This "growth spurt" can last for two or three years until we reach our adult height.

Arms and legs get longer and internal body organs get larger.

The overall body shape also changes.

Girls usually become curvier during this time; gaining weight on their hips, developing breasts and experiencing an increase in overall body fat. Breasts start to develop, and girls experience their first menstrual period.

Boys will see broader shoulders, stronger muscles and darker, more developed genitals as well as pubic hair. The larynx lengthens and the voice 'breaks' as it becomes deeper.

In females, breast development usually begins as a firm, tender lump under the center of one or both breasts, occurring on average at about ten-and-a-half years of age. Within six to twelve months, the swelling begins on both sides a year after that, the breasts are approach mature size and shape.　There is a lot of variation in the size and shape of female breasts.

Boys generally begin producing semen between the ages of twelve and sixteen[8]. Those spontaneous erections you love so much will start to occur more frequently (and probably less conveniently). Nocturnal emissions of sperm known as "wet dreams," may begin happening as well.

As girls sexually mature, their vaginas start lubricating when they are aroused. They also start having erotic dreams.

Another early sign of puberty in both sexes is hair growth. Hair grows under arms and pubic area. Boys will begin to grow hair on their faces. As puberty progresses, it will become thicker, darker and heavier and may grow on their chest as well.

The more unfortunate parts of puberty are:

Acne is caused by the hormones produced during puberty. These are minor infections also called pimples (or "zits") caused by skin pores becoming clogged with dirt and oils.

The simplest way to keep your pores clean is to wash your skin regularly and thoroughly with a cleansing product-not necessarily soap, which can dry out your skin, causing it to produce more oils in response.

Gel, cream or lotion containing Benzoyl Peroxide or Azelaic Acid, or a topical antibiotic may also be applied directly to the skin. Prescription oral treatments may also be required. If you are concerned about your acne, it is worth visiting your doctor or a dermatologist for an expert opinion.

Tips:

- Try not to touch your face too much.

- Try not to wash your face too much.

- Eat a good, balanced diet.

- Bathe at night, rather than in the morning.

- And wash your sheets – especially your pillowcases.

- Do not squeeze.

Body odor is created when bacteria and sweat in certain body areas – specifically underarms become fragrant.

Body Odor (or "B.O.") is normal for everyone, but it can be more intense for teens. Showering and carrying deodorant with you is very important. Everyone between eleven and twenty-one should be carrying extra "emergency deodorant" in their backpacks.

These things simply mean that the body is developing correctly during puberty.

Other common concerns and problematic behavior identified during puberty are things like:

- Depression

- Stress

- Risk-taking

- Mood swings

- Substance abuse

- Sexual feelings and activity

- Energy fluctuations

- School problems

When puberty starts, and how long it lasts, is affected by:

- Genetics (body shape and family history and size)

- Environment (altitude and nutrition, obesity vs. exercise, stress level etc.)

Everyone matures at their own pace, but we all end up in the same general place. However, if you have concerns about any of the above things, talk it over with your health care provider or parent.

Chapter 4

OTHER BODY ISSUES

Though not all of these things apply to guys – some of them affect the women in our lives – our moms, sisters, friends, maybe even girlfriends or, someday, daughters. It is a good thing for men to understand these things to provide the women in our lives some understanding and compassion.

Menstruation Is the shedding of blood and membrane, which would have formed the nourishing home for an embryo to grow into a fetus. If the lining is not used (if she does not get pregnant) her body cleans out the uterus by sloughing off the unused material in the form of a bloody discharge. Menstruation (also called a "period") is considered the beginning of a woman's menstrual cycle.

A menstrual cycle is the period between the start of one bleeding period and the start of the next bleeding period. Cycles typically last twenty-eight days, but can vary from woman to woman.

Females are most fertile (most likely to get pregnant) between day ten and day eighteen, when the lining of the uterus starts to thicken to prepare for the fertilized egg. Ovulation (the release of the egg from the ovaries) occurs around day fourteen. The egg moves down the fallopian tube and reaches the uterus two to three days later. If the egg is not fertilized by a sperm along the way, the thickened lining is shed, and another cycle begins.

Typically, first periods occur around age twelve or thirteen. However, some girls begin having periods as young as eight years old, others may not start until sixteen.[9] Once menstruation begins, it continues until menopause occurs (around the age of fifty) and monthly menstrual cycles end.

Some women never have regular cycles, but most females menstruate, on average, about five to seven days during each cycle.

It can be helpful for everyone to learn to track the cycle's of the important women in our lives. Looking for clues and signs about when our moms, sisters, female roommates and girlfriends are cycling, helps us prepare for their behavior (and emotional changes).

Premenstrual Syndrome (PMS) is a range of symptoms and effects that happen during the period between ovulation and menstruation. Most women (approximately 85%[10]) have some symptoms of PMS. These symptoms are usually predictable and occur regularly during the two weeks prior to menstruation. Generally, symptoms may vanish either before or after the start of menstrual flow.

The symptoms include:

- Cramps

- Abdominal pains

- Depression/ Crankiness/ Sadness

- Difficulty concentrating

- Sore breasts

- Weight gain (because the body retains water)

- Fatigue

- Headaches

- Cravings for specific foods

- Other medical issues such as headaches or asthma or allergies

The three most common symptoms are irritability, tension, and mood swings.

- Good guys do not hold ridiculous stereotypes about girls on their period.

- Good guys do not hold it against them.

- Good guys look for signs (like tampon packaging in the trash can).

- Good guys make a note on their calendar (with a day or two remind to give ourselves a heads-up so we are prepared for the emotional or behavior changes the women in our lives might go through).

- Good guys NEVER bring it up or ask "are you having your period?" (even when we are pretty sure they are.)

- Good guys have some compassion, and remind ourselves that if WE bled for three days without dying we would be crankier, stressed out and probably act differently too.

American culture, in particular, places strange emphasis on **Breast Size.**

Breast augmentation is the most popular cosmetic surgery in the United States, but the US Justice Department has spent $8,000 on curtains to hide the eighty year-old statue of a naked Lady Justice from the cameras during press releases.[11]

Girls are treated differently if they have large breasts and girls are treated differently if they have small breasts.

Large breasts are painful and awkward to deal with. Some girls with smaller breasts may feel inadequate. Breast implants get some women dates but it also shortens their life span and makes them statistically three times more likely to kill themselves.

Women are inundated for most of their lives about breast size with either idealized or unrealistic images. Not only are they pressured by other women, but by men as well.

As men we can help by keeping in mind that there is no male equivalent to cleavage. If what guys were packing behind their zippers was as focused on in the media, as emphasized by the clothes they were meant to wear or the first (or only) thing people stared at when they saw them, the world would be a very, very different place.

Women need to be comfortable with their bodies and find the strength to rise above the expectations and judgments that are made (sometimes by themselves) about their bodies – remembering that

- The ability to breast-feed

And

- The risk of breast cancer

– The two really most important things about breasts – are completely unrelated to size.

Speaking of size, a lot of guys can become obsessed with our penises… its habits, behaviors and size. A penis is the very first toy guys get and we play with it all our lives – we do target practice when we pee, we can write our names in the snow… a guy's penis is always there, and one of the few things that is just ours.

A shockingly large number of women have never even seen their own vagina, but a man and his penis are bonded, lifelong friends. Our penis is the first thing we notice in the morning and most of us nod off holding it and twitching our feet as we fall asleep at night. We protect our penis with our lives.

As weird or fun as this sounds, it also comes with a price.

One of those prices is **Boner Shame.**

There are scams in the world that prey on insecure guys' fears about the size of their penises. These include, pills or patches, exercises and weird suction-device-contraptions. None of these work by the way, other than one surgery, which severs the ligaments that anchor the base of your penis to your pelvis. This allows the penis to hang freely giving it the appearance of being longer – though it also gives the appearance of a cucumber hanging in a sock, which sacrifices stability and, sometimes, the ability to stay erect.

Most guys do not know or believe how big the average penis is. For most of us, the only penises (other than our own) we have seen, up close and personal were our father's, which were obviously bigger than ours at the time (and hopefully not erect). Also, the perspective with which we have seen our own penises is limited and nothing like what anyone else sees.

Yes, even that picture you took with your phone is a distorted image.

P.S. Stop doing that.

Outside of the locker room, where (again) the penises are not usually erect, the only other erect penises most guys have seen (besides their own) have been in porn. There is a reason that a lot of these guys are in the porn business – and it is not their acting ability. And a lot of the ones who have not been naturally endowed by the benevolent universe have had things done to them, like that scary, cucumber surgery I mentioned earlier.

Regardless of what they look like flaccid (soft), nine out of ten penises are basically the same length when erect (hard). The average erect penis is about six-and-a-half inches erect. But even this means essentially nothing, because chances are every guy reading this book has had a go with a ruler at some point, and only a handful would have measured it the exact same way each time.

Making things even more complicated, there are two different kinds of penises: **grow-ers and show-ers**.

A "show-er" is a long, soft penis that does not increase much in length as it becomes erect.

A "grow-er" is a shorter, soft penis that increases, sometimes doubling or tripling in length, as it gets erect. It is estimated that almost 80% of men are growers.[12]

Again, whether grow-er or show-er, most penises are about six-and-a-half inches erect.[13]

The typical vagina of a woman is only three inches long when not sexually excited and, when it is, is usually only an inch or so longer.[14] Likewise, the prostate is located only about three inches inside a guy's bum.

This means, pretty much any penis will fit pretty much any vagina or anus, unless you happen to be one of those rare guys with a penis length of less than four inches.

And even if you do have a smaller penis (or worry that you have one), being on the smaller side is an opportunity to get creative and good at all the other fun and sexy things that your partners tend to enjoy more than having your penis inside of them, anyway.

Being too large has its own limitations as well. Well-endowed guys are as self-conscious, and get their self-worth wrapped up in their penises just as much as the smaller-sized guys. Bigger guys can also have trouble finding condoms that fit, and can have trouble with partners trying to accommodate them – whether it's a vagina, an anus or even a mouth.

Bottom line: There is no normal when it comes to penis size or shape.

Bottom line: There is no normal when it comes to vagina size or shape.

Be happy with what you have and try to remember that satisfying sexual experiences (for most people) have very little to do with the size of the organ and a lot more to do with what (and who) you do with it.

Circumcision is a controversial surgical procedure in which the foreskin is cut off or removed from a penis. In some cultures, it is considered a religious ritual, symbolizing an outward sign of a compact with God. This procedure is most often done when boys are infants.

Non-religious circumcision in English-speaking countries arose in the mid 1800's, in a climate of negative attitudes towards sex – especially concerning masturbation. In the United States, the medical rationale for circumcision was originally to control "masturbatory insanity" – the idea that masturbation caused a whole bunch of various mental disorders and physical illnesses.[15]

Leading advocates of circumcision at the time were John Harvey Kellogg and his colleagues, Sylvester Graham and C.W. Post. These advocates also created Shredded Wheat®, Graham Crackers® and Corn Flakes® as bland, tasteless, snack and breakfast foods, that were designed to keep illness-causing sexual problems such as masturbation from happening.[16] They also believed that circumcision would be an effective way to eliminate masturbation in males.

Some of those ideas about masturbation and myths about sexuality still exist in our culture today.

Three popular studies in Africa in the last few years have claimed to show that it reduces the risk of HIV transmission, though there is criticism about the application of the information on places and people outside of Africa.[17]

The reality is that the United States has one of the highest rates of male circumcision and also one of the highest rates of HIV infection in the developed world[18], suggesting that circumcision is not helping. More research is obviously needed before circumcision should be considered a reasonable prevention for any sexually transmitted infection.[19]

According to the Centers for Disease Control (CDC), the circumcision rate in America has plunged to its lowest point since WWII at 33% in 2009[20] – with almost half of all baby boys being released from hospitals intact. The practice is relatively rare worldwide (approximately 16% in Britain[21]), and has become less and less popular in recent years as parents have come to see circumcision as a painful surgery that removes an integral part of the male sexual anatomy.

Whether man or woman, intact or cut, anyone who has (or may someday have) male children will have to make a decision. I encourage everyone to do their own research before making any decisions.

Smegma is comprised of bacteria, yeasts, stale urine and dead skin cells which can collect under the foreskin of uncircumcised males to form a white, cheesy substance. It starts to develop at an early age, and can occur all through the life of a guy who is not circumcised. It is not a problem for every intact guy, but it can be. Smegma that is allowed to build up can cause irritation and soreness.

Boys who have an intact foreskin should (or should have been taught how to) retract their foreskin (if they are older than six or seven) and wash underneath at least once a day.

Blue Balls refers to a localized pain in the testicles that can happen if blood flow to the penis (which makes it erect) lasts too long. The ache

- Is relatively minor
- Is experienced by most guys at some point
- Causes no damage
- Will eventually go away by itself (or can be taken care of once he ejaculates)

Some guys use this pain to try to persuade others to have sex with them.

Boys, fail to be that guy.

Everybody else, don't fall for it – he can take care of it himself, if you know what I mean.

You know what I mean.

Chapter 5

BODY IMAGE

Is the way we see ourselves in our minds and mirrors, and the ways we feel about what we see.

A negative body image is a a way of seeing ourselves that may not be true or that causes shame, anxiety or self-consciousness or that interferes with our relationships with ourselves and other people.

A positive body image is an acceptance of the unique qualities of our own bodies and a feeling of comfort and confidence with them. A positive body image may also be a distortion, but ideally we are seeing the many parts of our bodies for how they really are.

People have given time, energy and money and other value into physical appearance since the beginning of time. Most of us are more concerned with our appearance than we'd care to admit. Advances in medicine and technology as well as media have caused concern to sometimes shift into obsession.

Negative Body Image

What people see and how they react to their reflection in a mirror will vary according to:

- Sex
- Age
- Environment
- Sexual orientation
- Peer cultures
- Societal views in general
- Whether you're partnered or single
- What kind of childhood you had
- Whether you take part in sports
- Even what you watch on TV or what magazines or blogs you read.

Research on body image shows that women are much more critical of their appearance than men and much less likely to admire what they see in the mirror.

Guys, in general, have much more positive body images than women – and actually tend to over-estimate their attractiveness.[22] Notice I said "positive" body image, not "healthy." Some men looking in the mirror literally do not see flaws in their appearance (see above, re: positive distortions).

Most females' dissatisfaction has to do with areas below their belt; hips, waists and thighs.

When men are dissatisfied, their main focuses of concern are above the belt; stomachs, chests and hair.

Gay guys are more likely than straight guys to be unhappy with their reflection in the mirror.

Lesbians are likely to be more satisfied with themselves in the mirror than straight women.[23]

Warning signs of negative body-image include:

- Low self-esteem in general – specifically, a strong need to fit in.

- Depression

- Unrealistic body standards

- Excessive exercise

- Disordered eating habits

The two biggest eating disorders are Anorexia (starvation) and Bulimia (binging and purging).

More than a million Americans have eating disorders. The vast majority of them are girls[24]. Many eating disorders cause damage to hearts, throats, metabolism and bowels and 10% of eating disordered people die within ten years.[25]

It is extremely important to speak to your doctor if you have concerns about your body, if you find yourself not eating for long periods of time or if you make yourself throw up.

It is difficult to develop Anorexia or Bulimia or other disordered eating habits if you have a healthy level of self-esteem and a healthy body image. This helps us experience – but not internalize – society's socially sanctioned standards of beauty.

In our society, women are judged more often and more critically on their appearance than men. American standards of female beauty are higher and less flexible than men's.

Have you ever seen the hot husband/ unfortunate wife sitcom? Has any major news anchor ever cared or commented on what outfit or shoes a male senator has ever worn anywhere? The buffness of Michelle Obama's arms is an almost constant topic of conversation in women's magazines. You can find out how much Angelina Jolie weighs by standing in any grocery store checkout line, but not Brad.

And don't be fooled into thinking that this does not impact men as well – statistically, 10% of eating disordered people are male[28]. These issues are somewhat jokingly referred to as "Manorexia" or "Boylimia," but they do exist and are more dominant in people who were teased about their bodies as children and those who are overweight and/ or athletes.

Positive Body Image

Things you can do to create and maintain a positive body image for yourself and those around you include:

Focus on associating with people who are:

- Genuinely concerned about your health.
- Trustworthy

Give others compliments – this makes you feel good as well.

Learn how to take compliments.

Avoid perfectionism.

Set goals and meet them, to improve your trouble areas.

Exercise to relieve stress and keep us healthy.

Get involved… groups… clubs… teams… These expose you to more diverse people, allowing you to appreciate how different people can be.

Focus on things you do well.

Help others – this has an even greater impact on positive self-worth than giving compliments.

Remember that everybody is different.

Including you.

Be proud of that.

And if you can't find a way to do that on your own, **find a therapist** that will help you.

A SPECIAL NOTE ABOUT HYGIENE

Good hygiene is important for positive self-image and a healthy relationship with your own body.

It also becomes important if you want others to have a relationship with your body.

Things such as bathing, brushing and flossing, changing your underwear and socks and cleaning underneath your foreskin should be done everyday.

Shaving schedules can vary from guy to guy depending on your age, ethnicity etc. Once you become sexually active (especially if it is with a woman), it is important to maintain either a clean-shaven look or a longer (softer) beard – Beard-It or Bic-It, because razor burn is no fun for anyone.

Trimming your fingernails should be done on (at least) a weekly basis – more often if you work with your hands. Take a look at your nails-if you wouldn't want them on your skin or inside your body, why would you think your partner would?

If you are expecting (or hoping) for any kind of sexual contact, you should give each of these areas a once-over before you leave the house.

SECTION II – IDENTITY

Chapter 6

SEX VS. GENDER VS. ORIENTATION

One's **sex** (whether you are male or female) has to do with one's physical parts and biological status as man or woman. It is a reproductive category, referring to physical things – boy parts or girl parts.

One's **gender** (whether you are masculine or feminine) is a term that is often used to refer to ways that people act, interact, or feel about themselves, which are associated with boys/men and girls/women. This refers to how "guy-like" or "chick-like" you are, which may or may not be different from the kind of genitals you have."

One's **orientation** (whether you are gay, straight or bisexual) has to do with what sex you choose to be sexual with and its relationship to your own.

Sexual identity is about the plumbing with which you were born (or acquire later through surgery).

Gender identity refers to one's sense of oneself as male, female, or transgender.

Sexual orientation refers to one's sexual attraction to men, women, both or neither.

- Heterosexual means romantic or sexual attraction to someone of the opposite sex.

- Bisexual means there is some degree of attraction to both sexes.

- Homosexual means romantic or sexual attraction to someone of the same sex. Though gay is used to describe this, generally "gay" refers to a male who is attracted to another male, "lesbian" means a female who is attracted to another female.

People generally experience sexual identity, gender identity and sexual orientation as different things. While aspects of biological sex are the same across different cultures, aspects of sexuality and gender may not be.

There are many theories as to how sexuality develops, though the American Psychiatric Association, American Academy of Pediatrics, American Counseling Association, American Association of School Administrators, American Federation of Teachers, American School Health Association, Interfaith Alliance Foundation, National Association of School Psychologists, National Association of Social Workers, National Education Association and The World Health Organization agree that sexuality is no more a choice than ear shape or bad breath or musical ability or height is.[27]

Chapter 7

HETEROSEXUALITY

Heterosexuality is physical and/or emotional attraction to people of the opposite sex. When a man has a romantic or sexual relationship with a woman.

Heterosexuality is also called "being straight." A strange term that implies not only that that heterosexuality is the norm (which it is), but that anything that is NOT that is "bent".

Heterosexuality is the visibly predominant behavior with regard to sex, and (outside of assisted reproductive technology) the only way that our species can reproduce new generations.

Chapter 8

HOMOSEXUALITY

Homosexuality is physical and/or emotional attraction to people of the same sex. When a man has a romantic or sexual relationship with a man or a woman has a romantic or sexual relationship with another woman.

The term GLBTQ

Stands for

Gay
Lesbian
Bisexual
Transgender
and either
Queer (meaning "not-straight")
or
Questioning (meaning "haven't quite figured it out yet")

GAY MYTHS

- You can tell who is gay by the way they act.

- Gay people want to be the opposite sex.

- Only gay people get AIDS.

- Gay people are more likely to become child molesters.

- If someone is abused by someone of the same sex, they can become gay.

- Gay is contagious.

- Gay people choose to be gay.

- Gay people can choose to not be gay.

- Fantasies about someone of the same sex means you are gay.

- Sexual contact with someone of the same sex makes you gay.

Same-sex sex is a phenomenon and has been observed in hundreds of animal species[28]; mammals, sea life, birds and worms, including lions, dolphins and even killer whales. In fact, no species has been found in which homosexual behavior does not exist (with the exception of species that never have sex at all or that are hermaphroditic).

Some estimate that approximately 1.5% of the human population is homosexual[29], however this number is probably higher and, may be misleading. It does not take into account bisexuals (or anyone else who may not be gay, but are not straight), and the "1.5%" is most likely the only people who are comfortable with their homosexuality and out.

Out means that you are open about your sexuality and tell people you are gay or bisexual.

It is hard to estimate exactly how many people may be gay, but afraid to come out, have not come out yet and/or are bisexual.

Chapter 9

BISEXUALITY AND THE CONTINUUM

In 1948, Albert Kinsey created the Kinsey Scale[30], a questionnaire in the form of a continuum that served to rate a person's attraction and behavior with regard to sex.

OPPOSITE SEX   SAME SEX

ACTIVITY
(WHAT YOU HAVE ACTUALLY DONE)

1   2   3   4   5   6

ATTRACTION
(WHO YOU ARE PHYSICALLY ATTRACTED TO)

1   2   3   4   5   6

PASSION
(WHO YOU ARE EMOTIONALLY ATTRACTED TO)

1   2   3   4   5   6

Kinsey found that most people have both heterosexual and homosexual thoughts and feelings, that the majority of people engage in sex with people of both sexes at some point in their lives, and suggested that most people are some flavor of bisexual.

Most contemporary research agrees with this, describing sexual identity as being very fluid – a continuum scale rather than closed categories. The idea of sexuality as fluid also meshes with the general understanding that sexuality develops and can change in certain ways over a person's lifetime. Most people do not stay in the exact same place on the scale for their entire life.

Most sex educators tend to follow the general conclusions of Kinsey's, in which heterosexuality, bisexuality and homosexuality make up a sexual identity continuum.

On this continuum, most people, though they might gravitate to either the "gay" or "straight" poles, float somewhere in the middle, and many men and women experiment with same sex-sex at some point.

A SPECIAL NOTE ABOUT COMING OUT

Coming out is the process of accepting and being open about one's sexual orientation and gender identity – particularly when one's orientation is not straight.

The opposite of this is called closeted (not out) – as in "He is out of the closet."

The first stage is coming out to one's self. This may happen anytime between adolescence and adulthood.

Exploring and deciding where we are on the spectrum between straight and gay is everyone's right and responsibility.

Sexuality is a process that many people discover about themselves, often through what is called experimentation.

A SPECIAL NOTE ABOUT EXPERIMENTATION

Experimentation is a way that some people help sort out where they are on that spectrum by trying sexual things with people of both sexes.

Just as there are

- Chocolate and Vanilla people

- Cake and Pie people

- Xbox and Playstation people

- PC and Mac people

- Edward and Jacob people

We come to decisions about which sides of certain fences we stand on by jumping those fences and trying different things.

Many straight people have done sexual things with someone of the same sex.

Many gay people have done something sexual with someone of the opposite sex.

Some people, however, are tempted to justify and explain repeated sexual acts with people of the same sex, because they are afraid this makes them gay.

However, if you have experimented with someone of the same sex more than a handful of times in a relatively short amount of time (such as a summer, semester or that week at band camp), you aren't "experimenting" anymore. At this point you have moved into "exploring."

Cheesecake is the combination of rich-yet-light, creamy, sweet, cheese filling inside of a crunchy, buttery, graham cracker crust.

How many times do you think one needs to "experiment" with cheesecake before they decide they like it?

Exactly.

These behaviors themselves do not make someone gay or straight or anything in-between, but engaging in them is a way for us to figure out who we are. Exploring does not define you forever – any more than trying a new haircut, sport or genre of music. What you are "into" right now is different than it was five years ago, and it will change over time.

Like ear shape or bad breath, musical ability or height, it is most likely a combination of biology and environment.[31/32]

Biological influences on whether someone is Straight, Gay, both, neither or somewhere in between, include genes, prenatal hormones and the structure of the brain.

The environmental pieces can be more obvious in some ways and harder to pin down in others, social and cultural stigmas, religion, politics, media and laws get in the way of people being able to deal honestly with their own (and others') sexualities.

Things to consider if you think/ wonder/ worry or believe you are some flavor of not-straight?

- What do you fantasize about when masturbating?
- What pornography do you find yourself looking at?
- Are you bored or pretending interest in the opposite sex?
- Do you feel like you are acting or playing the part of a straight person?
- Have you experimented more than three times with someone of the same sex?

Gay thoughts, feelings and even acts do not make someone gay.

(Many gay adults have done sexual things with the opposite gender[33] – it didn't make them straight!)

Repetitive gay thoughts, feelings and even acts may mean you are not straight.

If this is the case, then it is a good idea to find someone to talk to.

Because the next stage is **coming out to others.**

Coming out, can seem unfair in the sense that straight people do not have to sit down with friends or loved ones to let them know that they like the opposite sex and then answer people's questions.

It is NOT necessary for people who are not straight to tell anyone specific or gory details about their sex lives or practices.

Though it is not unusual or unhealthy to keep aspects of our personal and sexual lives, private, fighting against who you are, pretending to be someone you are not and living a life in which you have to keep secrets or tell lies is exhausting and cannot be done for long periods of time without causing problems.

Coming out serves the purpose of allowing us to be ourselves – to act and speak freely about our day-to day lives without having to double-check or censor everything that comes out of our mouth.

The rules of coming out are very similar to that of a swimming pool...

First of all, **HAVE FUN**. Be proud and enjoy yourself, celebrate who you are and surround yourself with other people who want to do the same.

WEAR SUNSCREEN. Well, O.K., not sunscreen, but protect yourself. Safer sex with regard to not-straight sex can be different than what you have learned, been taught, seen, tried or even had to think about. Ask questions and inform yourself before you jump in and start swimming.

In fact, rather than jumping in, a good way to start the coming out process is to **WADE INTO THE POOL**. Opening up to one or two trusted friends or family members and slowly gathering support while you build your confidence.

NO RUNNING. Go slow. Be prepared for some people to be shocked and possibly upset-particularly parents, and be gentle with them. Most parents experience a range of reactions when a child comes out. These reactions can range from "Does this mean I will never get grandchildren?" to worrying about your safety to their own biases and prejudices from growing up in a different generation or culture. It is important to strive not take these reactions personally. Be patient and give each person you come out to a few days to digest the new information and invite them to ask questions (because they might not know how to or may be afraid of upsetting or offending you).

KEEP AN EYE OUT FOR OTHERS. Do not be surprised to hear a few "Me too's" (a few "Polo's" for your "Marco"), when you start coming out. It's hard to know who else is in the pool until you get your head under water.

SAFETY FIRST. Take care of yourself and surround yourself with resources and information, such as The It Gets Better Project or your school's Gay-Straight Alliance (GSA).

P.S. Straight guys: they are called Gay-Straight Alliances. If you are cool with the gays, have friends or family who are gay – then join up and show some support.

DON'T SPLASH those who are not in the pool. Be polite when coming out. It is NEVER cool to out someone else.

The coming-out process can help build self-esteem and a capacity for intimacy, but it can be very stressful – sometimes harming self-esteem or intimacy in the process.

Dealing with gay thoughts and feelings, let alone coming out is a difficult process because of isolation, societal stigmas that often come out of fear, bigotry and hatred.

Gay kids account for 30% of all teen suicides[34] and 30% of gays and lesbians report that they have attempted suicide at some point in their life[35].

Most gay people prior to the 1970's were closeted because of laws and fears of being mistreated, or victimized – it was even considered a mental illness until the mid-1970's[36]. There are still very few positive gay role models in the media or popular culture. Most of the time, they are portrayed as vacuous, feminine and comical – often the butt of jokes.

Today the same fears and risks remain, though it is much safer for someone to be out. Many gay people have to struggle because of negative stereotypes, media misinformation and fear, which is called homophobia.

A SPECIAL NOTE ABOUT HOMOPHOBIA

Homophobia is discrimination and fear against gay people.

- Hatred of gays and gay people comes from fear.

- Fear comes from ignorance.

- Ignorance is a lack of knowledge.

A lot of the fear involves people's reactions to their own gay thoughts and feelings-a dream about someone of the same sex, curiosity or wondering.

Homophobia is a social disease, like racism or sexism or other kinds of bigotry. It is unfair and too often becomes violent. This is called gay-bashing and is considered a hate crime[37] – just as if someone were victimized because of the color of their skin or their religious beliefs.

There are some important terms which are considered homophobic.

The biggest ones are

- "Fag" (or "Faggot")
- "Dyke"

And

- "Queer"

(Like "Nigger" and other slurs that have come before them), these words are designed to insult and humiliate people based on qualities they cannot control or change.

And it is never cool to shame, hate-on, tease or treat differently someone for something they have no control over.

(Also, like other slurs that have come before them), some minority groups have attempted to "take back" the terms, using them amongst and in reference to themselves as a way to lessen the impact and pain they are associated with.

(And still like other slurs that have come before them), it is only acceptable to use those taken back terms if you are "in the club." Like black guys calling one another "Nigga," or gay girls calling each other "Dyke." If you are not in a particular club (or close enough with someone who is to be invited to the picnic), using these terms is extremely insensitive, disrespectful and should be avoided.

> Like "Retarded," using "Gay" as an insult (as in: "that shirt is Gay," or "I hated that movie, it was so Gay.") should be considered a no-no.

People who use these terms as offensive labeling and insults should probably be avoided as well.

Though most educated therapists and researchers believe that sexual orientation is unchangeable, some people still believe the opposite - that conversion (also called reparative therapy) is possible and effective, because they believe that people choose their sexuality. They use prayer, counseling and sometimes drugs or shock therapy to "cure" gay people.

These techniques are never aimed at straight people.

Therapy can be helpful for people who are troubled by their sexuality or are struggling emotionally or socially, but according to the American Psychiatric Association, there is no evidence that any treatment can change a homosexual person's feelings for others of the same sex. There is no published, scientific evidence supporting the efficacy of reparative therapy as a treatment to change anyone's sexual orientation.[38]

Changing a person's sexual orientation is not simply a matter of changing behavior. It would require altering someone's emotional, romantic and sexual feelings as well as recreating one's entire self-concept and social identity. People can change their behavior, but not their internal experience. You can't catch gay or turn or un-turn gay.

Gay thoughts, feelings and even actions do not make you gay, but they can help us figure out who and what we are.

Self-identity and sexual orientation both form slowly over time and in the context of life experiences. Sexuality is very fluid and how a person identifies today is not necessarily how they did so in the past – or how they may so in the future.

No one should feel pressured to label himself or herself until they are ready, but it is important to find someone to talk to about any thoughts and feelings that may be troubling to you.

Talking to a trusted friend, adult or teacher is especially important if you have felt targeted, threatened, harmed or abused because of your orientation.

Chapter 10

ANDROGYNY AND THE CONTINUUM

Transgender is an umbrella term used to describe people whose gender identity (sense of themselves as male or female) or gender expression may differ from the body shape and parts they were born with. A girl born with boy parts would be an example of this.

Not everyone whose appearance or behavior is gender-atypical is a transgendered person.

Transsexuals are transgendered people who live (or wish to live) as members of the gender opposite of the sex they were born with.

Biological females who wish to live and be recognized as men are called female-to-male (FTM) transsexuals or transsexual men.

Biological males who wish to live and be recognized as women are called male-to-female (MTF) transsexuals or transsexual women.

Transsexuals can seek medical interventions, such as hormones and surgery, to make their bodies as congruent as possible with their gender. The process of transitioning from one gender to the other is called sex reassignment or gender reassignment.

Usually people who are attracted to women prior to transition generally continue to be attracted to women after transition, and people who are attracted to men prior to transition continue to be attracted to men after transition. That means, for example, that a biological male who is attracted to females will be attracted to females after transitioning, and she may regard herself as a lesbian, though the sexuality of a transsexual can be as fluid as anyone else's.

Transvestites or cross-dressers wear the clothing of the opposite sex. They vary in why and how much they dress. Some cross-dress to express cross-gender feelings, some for fun, others for emotional comfort or sexual arousal. The majority of cross-dressers are straight males. Transvestites may or may not also identify as transgendered.

Drag queens (males) and drag kings (females) live part-time as members of the other sex primarily as performers – singing and/or dancing. Many drag performers identify as gay or lesbian and may or may not identify as transgender.

Other categories of transgender people include **androgynous and gender-queer** people. Exact definitions of these terms are difficult, but often include a sense of blending or alternating genders. Some people who use these terms to describe themselves see traditional concepts of gender as unnecessary.

An **androgynous** person either

- does not fit cleanly into typical masculine and feminine roles

and/or

- is able to draw from both traditionally masculine and feminine qualities.

Those who identify as **Gender queer** may think of themselves as

- being a third sex-both male AND female

and/or

- falling completely outside the gender binary as genderless (or agender) – being neither male nor female

In all of the above cases, pronouns should not be based on the shape of one's genitals, but on what the person inside of them prefers to be called.

Intersex

In humans, there are no actual "hermaphrodites." The word "hermaphrodite" is misleading, considered stigmatizing and should not be used. Though some intersex people do reclaim and use this term to describe themselves, it is not an appropriate term in general.

The preferred term for someone with atypical combinations of features that are usually considered either male or female is intersexed.

An intersexed person

- may have biological characteristics of both the male and female sexes

- may be chromosomally (internally) one sex, while physically (externally) another

or

- may have biological sex characteristics which cannot be classified as either male or female.

PART THREE: THE OTHER INS AND OUTS

SECTION III – RELATIONSHIPS

Chapter 11

RELATIONSHIPS

**When it comes to relationships,
Hardly anyone is taught…**

…How to ask someone out

The best way to meet someone is to:

- Go to a place where there are other people doing something you already know you enjoy. The concert of a band you like, a friend's performance, a class about something that interests you…

- Do interesting things that others would want to hear or talk about. Like reading a popular book in a coffee shop or at lunch or joining a group or team of some kind.

- Do research to familiarize yourself with things that the person/people you like are interested in.

Note: it is legitimate to ask someone out via text message, though you score points for bravery, class, vulnerability and romance if you can cowboy-up and do it in person.

A SPECIAL NOTE ABOUT SMALL TALK

Small Talk is made up of a very simple, formula.

Statement = make a comment

Disclosure = reveal something personal about yourself

Invitation = ask a (not "Yes" or "No") question

Eventually you want to indicate interest in a straightforward way.

Issue a VERY SPECIFIC invitation.

- "I'm thinking about going to see _____ on Saturday afternoon, would you like to come with?"

Is better than,

- "Do you want to go out sometime?"

…How to let someone know you are interested

It never hurts to get to know people as friends first – it can make dating a lot less stressful and a lot more interesting.

Other tips:

- Smile.
- Say "Hello".
- Speak to them like a relative you actually like.
- Make eye contact – hold your gaze one second longer than what is comfortable for you, then look away.
- The second time you make eye contact – smile again.

- Ask open-ended questions. (That means questions the other person can't answer with just a "Yes" or a "No".)

- Keep the conversation flowing (If they are interested, they will help you do this).

Learn to spend time alone. It's hard to find someone who wants to spend time with you if you can't do it yourself.

Learn to pay attention to the kinds of people you are interested in… how they make you feel, how they treat you, etc. You are half of all the relationships you are in, and making sure we are aware of any of our negative patterns is important to help make sure we are choosing people who are making us happy.

A SPECIAL NOTE ABOUT FLIRTING

Flirting is fun, sexy and boosts both people's egos.

Sexual harassment is not fun or sexy, and only boosts one person's ego.

The line between the two can be crossed when:

- It is one-sided.

- It focuses on the other person's body rather than the other person.

- There is a power differential.

- It is done in the workplace.

- If one person becomes embarrassed, creeped-out, insulted or scared.

- If you are doing or saying something you would not do in front of other people.

- If you are doing or saying something you would be upset about if someone did it to you (or someone you care about).

...How to know when someone is interested back

Good signs from her:

- A smile that shows teeth.

- Touching of you of any kind.

- An out loud laugh.

- Primping in general, but specifically anything involving her lips or hair.

- An introduction to her friends.

Good signs from him:

- A smile that shows teeth.

- Touching of you of any kind.

- An out loud laugh.

- Touching himself in any obvious place.

- A look back after you pass each other.

A SPECIAL NOTE ABOUT DATING

Whether man or woman, your first date should be fun, light and public.

- To avoid uncomfortable first date situations, try to "meet there,"

- If you are meeting there, be five minutes early.

- If you are picking your date up, be five minutes late.

- Not ten.

- Have plenty of cash to cover the bill.

- Arrive early to get comfortable and relaxed.

- Be willing (and prepared) to talk about yourself and ask the other person questions. Politics, money, religion and exes are off limits in terms of topic-matter.

- Be honest, be polite, be yourself and expect nothing more at the end of the date than a kiss on the cheek.

Other tips:

- Dating is expensive; it costs money, time and emotions. If you're not able or willing to spend these things, then keep masturbating.

- If you're not going to call – don't say you will.

- If you say will, then do it within two days.

- If anything physical happens that couldn't be shown on the Disney Channel – call the next day.

- Make sure there's been at least one Saturday night date by date three.

…How to let someone know you are not interested

Stereotypically, it is the boys' job is to ask. The girls' job is to decide to say "yes" or "no". Both jobs are equally difficult. If the other person is not making the situation more stressful, than neither should you.

No one likes to be rejected-if you're not interested, be nice about it.

How do you let someone of the same sex know if you are uninterested? The same way you would let someone who is of the opposite sex – this should NEVER include insults, threats or violence of any kind.

Typical men pick fights or turn into jerks until the other person breaks up with them, Don't be that guy. Real men speak their minds, and let the other person do the same. They are honest, non-violent and accept responsibility for the choice themselves (instead of trying to place blame on the other person).

When you must break up with someone, do it :

- Quickly

- As humanely as possible

- In service to the kind of relationship you want to have with them afterward.

BTW, People notice those guys who can't be friends with ANY of the people they have dated before.

Breaking up with someone is different than asking someone out (see above re: bravery and class). **If you have seen someone's underwear then you must break up in person.** Breaking up with someone via text is both cowardly and lame – fail to be that guy.

…How to know if a relationship is good for you

A general list of aspects of relationships are below.

There are many other things that factor into relationship, but this list may be a good place to start thinking about the relationships you are in.

Use this list to help to figure out how healthy/ unhealthy these things are in terms of the relationships you are (or want to be) in. This is ongoing work in a relationship.

- Respect
- Honesty
- Trust
- Fairness
- Talking/ Listening
- Boundaries
- Needs
- Support
- Love
- Sex

In healthy relationships, there are sometimes unhealthy behaviors that can be improved. Partners can talk about them and work on them. But sometimes relationships are unhealthy and sometimes even the healthy relationships cannot be fixed.

The goal is to know which of these relationships you are in.

Good boyfriends do not:

- Stop their partners from having other friends.

- Control all of the decisions in the relationship.

- Give their partners orders.

- Spy on their partners/ snoop through their phones or email.

- Ever put their hands on their partners out of anger.

- Force, trick, bribe, bug or guilt anyone into doing anything sexual they do not want to do.

(Good girlfriends don't do these things either).

Chapter 12

COMMUNICATION

Rule Number One: If you can't talk about it you shouldn't be doing it.

"It" can be defined as:

- Names of body parts.

- Names of certain sexual acts.

- Your body.

- Your past sexual behavior.

- Definitions of sex or virginity.

- Your previous partners.

- Safer sex methods.

TIPS FOR GOOD COMMUNICATION

A large chunk of communication is what comes out of your mouth.

- I statements

Which means starting sentences with "I think", "I feel", and "I want". This can help to make yourself clear and can avoid putting other people on the defensive (Like when you start out saying "You…").

- Open-ended questions

Which encourage people to talk and continue the conversation ("What are you upset about…" or "what do you think of…') instead of stopping ("Are you still mad?" "Do you wanna…?").

Another big chunk of communication is what goes in your ears.

Listening to others makes them more likely to listen back. People have a hard time knowing you listened to them unless you show them.

Listen between the words and try to figure out what the other person thinks and feels. When you think you have it figured out, let them know by

- Asking clarifying questions

Which means clearing up any confusing parts or words of what they just said.

- Paraphrasing.

Which means restating what they just said in a different way to make sure/ show them that you understand.

Show your partner that you respect her/him enough to ask about his/her sexual needs and desires. If you are not accustomed to communicating with your partner about sex and sexual activity, the first few times may feel awkward. But, practice makes perfect.

The more times you have these conversations with your partner, the more comfortable you will become communicating about sex and sexual activity.

Your partner may also find the situation awkward at first, but over time you will both be more secure in yourselves and your relationship.

Ideally, sexual behavior between two people should be viewed as teamwork. You are in this together and if it is more difficult to have a conversation with your partner about sex than it is to actually do the sex – that is a good sign that you should probably wait a bit longer.

A SPECIAL NOTE ABOUT TECHNOLOGY

Communication is the most important factor in relationships.

A lot of communication these days occurs via technology.

Relationships that occur only between screens are not actual relationships.

Issues such as emotional expression, body language and intuition are very important in healthy relationships – especially as a relationship grows closer to becoming sexual.

One cannot read a facial gesture, know when you have fallen into that sweet-spot of hesitation right before a kiss, or how to tell if it's O.K. to put your hand on someone's butt via text message.

Balance your screen relationships with actual, real-time, human contact.

Do not say or do anything in a text message that you would not say or do if the person was standing in the room in front of you. (This includes showing them your penis.)

SECTION IV – SEXUAL ACTIVITY

Chapter 13

SEXUAL AROUSAL

Humans do not have a mating season like other animals on the planet, though sexual arousal and response is a cycle in both men and women.

The human arousal cycle has four basic parts:[39]

Excitement (or arousal) is the Horny part.

- The interest in sex and sexual behavior

- Feeling attracted to someone

or

- Feeling actively turned on

The body responds to this by increased temperature and blood flow. Blood flows specifically to the genitals creating erections in men and moisture for women. During male arousal, blood flows into the spongy erectile tissue inside the penis, causing it to elongate and becomes erect (getting hard). Female arousal starts the swelling of the areas around the vagina, erection of the clitoris and nipples, and secretion of lubricating fluids in the vagina (getting wet).

Stimulation of the genitals through friction causes the nervous system to fire up sensory receptors in the penis, vaginal walls, anus and clitoris. The sperm leave the testicles and join secretions of other glands to form semen.

Plateau is the highest point of sexual excitement.

- Being actively engaged in sexual activity.

Orgasm is the peak of the plateau stage and the point at which sexual tension is released, creating waves of pleasurable sensations as well as muscular contractions of the penis (male) or vagina (female) and anus (both), which eventually end in intense feelings called orgasm, often accompanied by ejaculation. Ejaculation is also called "coming," as well as many other things.

It is important to note that orgasm and ejaculation are not the same thing.

- Orgasm is the big, good feeling.
- Ejaculation is the discharge of fluids.

Both men and women orgasm.

Although they are similar, there are differences between the male and female orgasm.

Men reach orgasm most typically through the rubbing of their glans, but can also reach orgasm through stimulation of their prostate.

Some women reach orgasm through vaginal penetration (which can be intercourse, though usually involves stimulation of the G-Spot), but almost 80% also need clitoral stimulation to achieve orgasm[40].

Orgasms from stimulation of the glans or clitoris, tend to focus in (picture the Death Star's laser at the beginning of Star Wars).

Orgasms through stimulating the G-Spot or prostate tend to focus outward (think of the Death Star blowing up at the end of Star Wars).

Both men and women ejaculate.

Some women emit fluid from their urethra during orgasm and this is called female ejaculation. There is a female counterpart to the male prostate, technically known as "Skene's" gland, embedded in the wall of the urethra. Just like the male prostate, the ducts from these glands crate secretions in women.

This fluid's primary purpose is the lubrication of the vagina. It is similar to semen (without sperm), and some women can actually expel (or ejaculate) this liquid.

Men ejaculate semen (also called "come" or "cum"), the combination of sperm and other liquids gathered along the way. The average guy ejaculates about a teaspoon of fluids.

Each teaspoon contains approximately 600 million spermatozoa[41]. There are so many of them because sperm are very sensitive; they are easily damaged and affected by heat, time, and the acidity of both the urethra and the vagina. In the end, less than 1000 sperm make it to the egg. Typically, just one gets in.

Resolution is the body returning to its normal unexcited state blood flow returns to normal and genital excitement subsides. This tends to happen fairly quickly after orgasm.

During this stage, the genitals may become extremely sensitive, ticklish or even painful to the touch. This sensation is part of the resolution and will pass rather quickly.

The refractory period is the time between when someone has an orgasm before they can have another one. Women tend to be able to do this much faster than men.

Chapter 14

SEXUAL ACTIVITY

People's sexual likes, dislikes and needs are as different as our personalities.

What someone really likes, another may not. What one person is excited about may be scary to another.

Our choices are greatly influenced by myths and misinformation we get from media, television, music, movies and the Internet. These things might have some people believing that men need to be aggressive, women are supposed to be passive, that men are supposed to have ten-inch penises and that women should enjoy it when they do. (By the way, in both cases, most do not).

We are taught to believe that people scream and moan during sex and do it in places like bathtubs. We are taught that everyone knows what they are doing, that they do it for forty-five minutes and orgasm (at the same time as their partner of course) every time.

Orgasm does not have to be the whole point of a sexual experience.

Orgasm does not mean that everything went right, and everyone got what they wanted.

Not having an orgasm does not mean that something went wrong.

There's plenty of fun to be had without that big finish.

This usually makes more sense to girls than boys, because it sounds like Disneyland without the Matterhorn or playing football without any touchdowns, but keep in mind that our largest sexual organ is our skin.

Sex is an urge human animals have – not a lot different than eating or sleeping[44]. There are different kinds of sexual intercourse and activity. This is because the drive is not voluntary but the behavior is. Like eating – we need to eat for survival, but some people eat veggies and brown rice and some eat fast food five times a week.

There are no universal positions or patterns that work for everyone.

Again,

There is nothing wrong with making yourself feel good or enjoying making someone else feel good as long as:

- You are comfortable with what you are doing.

- You are doing it safely.

- You are doing it legally.

- You are aware of the consequences.

and

- No one (including yourself) is getting hurt.

Chapter 15

MASTURBATION

AKA: manual sex, beating off, whacking off, jerking off, jacking off (jilling off for the girls) and hundreds of other terms.

Masturbation is sexual stimulation or rubbing (usually) of one's own genitals, to achieve sexual arousal – (usually) to the point of orgasm. Stimulation can also be performed by other people, by objects or by other types of bodily contact.

Most guys masturbate by rubbing their penis with either a closed fist or an open palm. Some guys use lubrication and others prefer a dry hand. This should, obviously, be done in private, such as your bedroom or the bathroom. Some guys also hump blankets or pillows.

Guys can masturbate lying in bed, sitting in a chair or standing in the shower. You can catch your semen in the palm of your hand, let it land on your stomach while lying on your back or wash down the drain in the shower.

Along those lines, the only generally accepted places to masturbate are in your room or the bathroom.

Remember, a gentleman always keeps the door closed.

Strive to not to leave the faucet running for long periods of time – the Earth is in terrible shape as it is, we could all die.

Avoid public places, like at school, in your car or anywhere near a webcam.

At home, avoid other people's bedrooms, and your living room (would you like realizing that earlier that day someone else was doing that in your bed or sitting naked on your couch with their dick in one hand and the remote in the other?).

Cleanup is important. A box of tissue next to your bed is a good idea, though some guys prefer a towel, or a pair of socks in those moments.

Along those same lines, if you are old enough to masturbate, you are old enough to start doing your own laundry – it should not be anyone else's job to clean up your dry, crusty messes.

A SPECIAL NOTE ABOUT WET DREAMS

Many guys experience nocturnal emissions, more commonly known as "wet dreams." A wet dream is when a build-up of sperm is spontaneously ejaculated while a guy is sleeping. This sometimes happens while we are dreaming about sex, though not necessarily.

Wet dreams may wake you up, or you may find a sticky or crusty mess under your sheets in the morning. As with masturbating, it is the mannerly thing to do to make sure that no one other than yourself cleans up your mess.

Not everyone has wet dreams, and those who do have fewer and fewer as they begin masturbating and grow older.

Some people do not masturbate, though most do – both males and females. It is estimated that approximately 95% of men and almost 90% of women masturbate.[43/44] Masturbation often begins in adolescence and continues through adulthood.

Though most people masturbate at some point in their lives, it is not a common topic of conversation for most people.

The word itself is hundreds of years old and Latin in origin: "masturbare" – a combination of two Latin words, manus (hand) and stuprare (defile)[45]. So the word meant, basically, to pollute yourself with your hand. This created a built-in association of shame and uncleanliness, which has carried into modern times. Masturbation is still associated with guilt and anxiety – mostly due to people not understanding the fact that masturbation is not harmful and partly due to centuries of religious teaching that it is sinful.

Many people have received negative messages about masturbation from our parents or know someone who was "caught" masturbating.

Has anyone ever heard of someone being "caught" brushing their teeth?

Masturbation is often the topics of insults, gross-out jokes and teen comedy movies, which can also cause guilt and confusion.

So to be clear:

Masturbation

- Does not make you blind
- Does not make you gay
- Does not make you deaf
- Does not make you crazy
- Does not make you grow hair on your hands
- Does not make you run out of sperm
- Does not make you stupid
- Does not make you or anyone around you die
- Does not make you sick
- Does not make you a loser

Masturbation is a natural and harmless expression of sexuality in both men and women and a perfectly good way to experience sexual pleasure without the risks of pregnancy or disease.

Masturbation

- Does release sexual tension

- Does reduce stress and can help you sleep[46]

- Does help you become more comfortable with your own body, sexuality and fantasy life – making you better prepared for sexual activity with a partner later.

- Does make for a fun alternative to intercourse with a partner, reducing your chance of pregnancy and disease.

Bottom line: there is nothing wrong with you if you masturbate.

In fact the only time masturbation can be harmful is when it becomes compulsive – when it takes up so much of your thoughts, time and energy, that it starts to cause problems in other areas of your life.

This is also an argument against pornography, as the two things are unfortunately linked on a fairly regular basis – especially for guys.

Compulsive masturbation and/or pornography use (like all other compulsive behaviors) is a sign of an emotional problem and needs to be addressed by a counselor.

A side note guys: avoid **The Death Grip** – masturbating too quickly and/or with a very tight grip.

This can lead to premature ejaculation, which is no fun for anyone. Coming quickly may have served you when you were first masturbating and afraid of mom or dad walking in, but big boys need to learn how to take their time.

- Practice masturbating for longer periods of time.

- Masturbate WITHOUT pornography.

- Masturbate with condoms on to get used to the feel.

- Learn other fun things to do besides insertion that make your partners feel good.

A SPECIAL NOTE REGARDING PORNOGRAPHY

Supreme Court Justice Potter Stewart once famously said, "I know it when I see it."[47]

According to TopTenReviews online, every second, 28,258 Internet users are viewing pornography. A total of seventy-two million adults visit pornography websites monthly.[48]

A 2009 study from the Universite' De Montreal (funded by the Interdisciplinary Research Center on Family Violence and Violence Against Women) attempted to examine the effects of pornography on men.

They needed two groups of men over the age of twenty; one group who used pornography and one that didn't.[49]

But they couldn't find any who did not consume pornography.

The research concluded that most boys seek out pornographic material by the age of ten, when they are most sexually curious, and by age twenty, statistically every guy has viewed pornography.

They also found that 90% of pornography is consumed on the Internet. On average, single men watch pornography three times a week for fourty minutes. Those who are in committed relationships watch it on average 1.7 times a week for twenty minutes.

So, porn does not turn men into perverts or rapists any more than showing straight porn to gay people makes them straight.

HOWEVER…

Media does impact the ways that we look at (and operate in) the world.

Pornography is designed to sexually excite people, it is also designed to be addictive – this is a typical marketing ploy, which works very well.

Viewing pornography on a regular basis can have harmful and damaging effects – especially during adolescence when we are forming who we are and what we are aroused by.

Pornography:

- Can become a (very poor) substitute for sexual education.

- Portrays unrealistic ideas of sexual interaction.

- Can distract from actual relationships.

- Can lead to negative imprinting/ deviant arousal to unhealthy or illegal things.

- Can weaken or atrophy one's own imagination and capacity for fantasy.

- Can be addictive.

- Can be expensive.

Like substance use, choosing to incorporate pornography into an existing sexual lifestyle as an adult is different than creating a sexual lifestyle that stems from pornography.

You wouldn't assume you knew how to drive after playing Grand Theft Auto, would you?

DO NOT USE PORN AS SEX ED.

Chapter 16

KISSING

No one seems to be quite clear about how or why touching our lips to someone else's came to be.

Though there are many theories, we know that people have been locking lips with each other for centuries, with references found as early as 1500 B.C.[50]

We do know that, the modern, romantic kiss is one of the few sexualized acts which involve all five senses; sight, sound, smell, touch and taste.

Kissing is also incredibly intimate, feels good, evokes passion and creates a physical connection between ourselves and our partners.

The basic steps of a kiss are:

- Eye contact

- Slightly parted lips

- And a tilt of the head so your noses don't hit (Note: twice as many people tilt to the right rather than the left[51]).

Opening the mouth and putting your tongue in the other person's mouth (or letting them do that to yours) is commonly called French kissing or "making out".

Learn how to do this, and do it well. That doesn't mean wagging your tongue around like a dog out a window or trying to suck someone's ribs up their neck.

The correct ratio is one minute of tongue for every three minutes of no – tongue.

Other tips for kissing:

- Proceed carefully with eyeglasses and braces.

- Fresh breath and a clean mouth are very good things (although two garlics/ two coffees/ two orange-mango smoothies generally cancel each other out…)

- And smoking is a kissing no-no (you shouldn't be doing that anyway).

You can catch certain infections as well as the common cold from kissing, but most people would agree that kissing is worth it.

Hickeys are bruises caused by sucking blood to the surface of the skin. The bruising can last from a couple of days to a couple of weeks.

Most people give hickeys as a way of marking their territory. Giving hickeys are generally seen as immature, very "middle-school" and should never, ever be done to anyone without consent.

The social issues around hickeys revolve around embarrassment and getting in trouble with your parents, not to mention having a hickey can make you look (very publicly) like someone who does not make good choices. There is a relatively small percent of the population that thinks hickeys are cool or funny.

Fail to be that person.

…And don't let the ones who are anywhere near your neck.

Chapter 17

FOREPLAY AND AFTERPLAY

All the fun, lovey, gropey stuff you do before and after the ACTUAL sex is just as important (and can be just as fun) as the ACTUAL sex. This stuff is called Foreplay (when it happens before the sex), and Afterplay (when it happens afterward).

This can range from conversation, to cuddling, to kissing, to contact with the more than a dozen pleasure spots on the body other than the genitals called erogenous zones.

They include the genitals, but there are many more sensitive areas of the body that can make touching feel very sexy.

- The scalp

- Hair

- Ears

- Lips

- The neck

- Collar bones

- Shoulders

- Underarms

- Nipples

- Belly buttons

- Wrists

- Hips

- Lower back

- Perineum (the small area between his balls and his anus – also called the 'Taint')

- Testicles

- Back of the knee

- Toes

Take your time. Hit them all. Mix it up. Try to find a new one-everyone's body and response is different.

Regarding foreplay,

When a penis is ready for sex, it is obvious and happens quite quickly. This is not true for the ladies.

A vagina getting wet can take quite a bit more time than it takes for a penis to get hard. It is important that you are patient, check to see if she is ready and even help her along.

Anuses do not have the natural lubrication that vaginas do, and much more time and prep is needed before someone's butt is ready for sex (see **Anal Sex** below).

Manual and oral sex can play a big part of foreplay, a lot of women report having an easier and more pleasurable time with intercourse, if they have already had an orgasm.

Regarding afterplay,

It does not need to last nearly as long as foreplay might, but it is a great way to express the range of feelings that can happen after two people have sex with each other.

Though you might be tempted to turn on the T.V., grab a snack or fall asleep after the sex, spending even just a few minutes cuddling, kissing or talking can help you communicate about thoughts and feelings that are harder to say in other situations, just connect for a few minutes or maybe start round two…

Chapter 18

ORAL SEX

Oral sex is when one person puts their mouth or tongue on the genitals of another.

When this is done on a woman, this is called cunnilingus, and is sometimes referred to as "eating her out" (even though there is no actual biting involved).

The clitoris is the part, that most women pay most attention to during masturbation. The tiny head of the clitoris is similar to a penis (and also called the glans), though the glans of a clitoris can contain even more nerve receptors than the glans of a penis.

On a male oral sex is called fellatio, but is more typically called a "blow job" (even though there is no actual blowing involved).

The frenulum is the part that most guys focus on when they are masturbating. The frenulum is the sensitive area under the head of the penis.

Guidelines for performing oral sex on a guy,

- No teeth!

- Don't be afraid to use your hands.

- Hint: all those people who teach how to give a blow job using bananas should be using ice cream cones instead…

- Deep-throating, in most cases, is a myth. It rarely ends well. Do not try.

- And don't forget the balls, they are there to play with-jiggle (don't squeeze), tug (don't pull) and stroke (like the top of a cat's tail, not the back of a dog's ear)

Guidelines for performing oral sex on a girl,

- Do not go straight for the clitoris.

- Tongues hurt unless they are lubricated.

- Do not wag your tongue about like a dog out a window.

- Spelling the alphabet with your tongue (or her name or the lyrics to your favorite Beatles' tune) is fun for everyone.

- Use your fingers as long as you keep your nails short and clean.

- BTW, keep your nails short and clean – stop reading and look at your hands – if you wouldn't want those hands touching YOUR gentles, then neither will she.

- A lot of women enjoy vaginal intercourse more if they have an orgasm first.

For everyone,

- Ask for feedback.

- Give feedback.

- Reciprocate. Reciprocate. Reciprocate – Do not ask anyone to put their mouth anywhere that you are not willing to put yours.

Boys tend like it a bit harder and faster as they get closer to the finish line.

Girls tend to like the exact. Same. Thing.

Chapter 19

PIV

Penis-in-vagina sex involves a man and a woman moving so that his erect penis moves in and out of her lubricated vagina.

PIV can be done from several positions. Boy and girl face-to-face is the most common and is referred to as the Missionary Position. Either person can be on top.

When he is on top, he is often supporting his own weight with his arms, while she lies underneath him with her knees bent or wrapped around him. This allows for both people to negotiate the depth of penetration, as well as allowing his pubic bone to rub against hers, stimulating her clitoris.

This position does not need to be considered standard, but it is popular, mostly because this particular position is the position that gives the most amount of skin-to-skin contact as well as allows for both eye contact and the ability to kiss. It's also the one seen most often in mainstream media, television and movies.

This position is also the best for couples trying to get pregnant as the deep penetration helps the sperm reach the cervix in the back while her lying on her back helps the semen pool around the opening of the cervix – making it more likely that sperm will enter. This position is helpful for her because she can relax in a way she can't with some other positions.

When she is on top, she can better control the depth of penetration and can also help his penis hit her G-spot. This position allows her to masturbate herself while being penetrated.

Most women require clitoral stimulation as well as penetration to achieve orgasm during vaginal sex.[52]

Despite what movies tell us, it is sometimes difficult and not always necessary to orgasm at the same time as your partner.

That being said, PIV, like most sex acts, should be safe and pleasurable for both people involved.

Ask questions along the way, listen to what your partner says and let her take the lead. Just because you may be on top does not mean you should be the one in charge.

Chapter 20

ANAL SEX

Anal sex is when a guy puts his penis into the anus of another man or a woman.

Anal sex is not a gay thing.

Only 50-80% of gay guys engage in anal sex.[53]

According to the National Survey of Family Growth, it is a regular feature in approximately a third of heterosexual couples.[54]

A 2008 study out of the Bradley Hasbro Children's Research Center found that more than half of fifteen to nineteen year olds have oral sex and that anal sex is increasing among straight teenagers and young adults (in fact between 1995 and 2004, it doubled).[55]

Straight kids participate in anal sex:

- To avoid pregnancy
- To please a partner
- To preserve their virginity ("saddlebacking")[56]

There are not many places in the human body with more nerve receptors than the anus.

This doesn't count the guys' prostates. The prostate is a small mini-doughnut-like gland about three inches inside a guy's butt and toward the front wall (think, toward the belly button). When the prostate is bumped by a finger, penis or some other object it makes anal sex done to a man very pleasurable,[57] and many people believe it to be similar to the G-spot in women.

In general, the person being penetrated during anal sex is referred to as the "bottom." The penetrator is the "top."

Girls do not have prostates.

There is no real need to go in any further than the front door (or back door, so to speak). Some women enjoy anal sex, though often is it a "gift" to their boyfriends. Anal sex for women is best when there is clitoral stimulation at the same time. She can do this herself or you can help her. Typically, anal sex should stop after she orgasms, as it becomes much less fun/ more painful at that point. (Yes, even if you're not finished!)

As with oral sex, it is important to reciprocate – anyone who wants to stick something up someone else's butt should be willing to have the same thing done to them. This creates empathy – helping you to be as gentle and safe with your partner as they are with you. Plus, as I said, anal sex, by design, is more pleasurable for guys than for women.

A man being penetrated in some way by a female partner is referred to as **pegging**.

Putting a mouth on someone's anus is called analingus, but is more commonly referred to as **rimming**.

Any of these acts can be considered fun, gross or whatever, depending on whom you ask.

What some people frown upon, many others enjoy as regular, sexual expression.

Whether or not you agree with these or are interested in them, these alternatives do avoid the problem of pregnancy, though there are still risks of disease and danger…

Anal intercourse is not something to be done spontaneously.

The reality is that

- The lining of the rectum is thin, easily damaged and can allow the HIV virus to enter the body.[58]

- The anus is not very well lubricated, so it is important to use some other form of lubricant to make sure that the person being penetrated isn't injured in some way

- Condoms are more likely to break during anal sex than during vaginal sex.
- The risk of contracting other STI's is higher for anal sex than oral sex as well.

According to the Centers for Disease Control, the probability of the receptive partner (the bottom) catching HIV during unprotected oral sex with an HIV carrier is one per 10,000 acts.

In vaginal sex, it's 10 per 10,000 acts.

In anal sex, it's 50 per 10,000 acts.

This means, anal sex is

5 times more dangerous than vaginal sex,

and

50 times more dangerous than oral sex.[59]

So some safety guidelines are necessary if you are going to try anal sex:

- In slow.
- Out slow.
- If you think it's going to hurt, it will.
- Relaxation is not the only requirement for a good experience.
- Slowing down, being gentle and using plenty of lube help avoid both the pain and trauma that can result from improperly attempted, anal sex.
- Stretching is a big part of the prep – start with fingers first…
- Nothing sharp – including and especially fingernails.
- Make sure anything that goes in will come out – things can be easily stuck.
- Stop when there is pain.
- The bottom (the one being penetrated) is the one in charge.

- Never go ass to mouth – (Hepatitis is a great concern, as are intestinal parasites).

- Along those same lines, never go ass to gyne either – there is a lot that happens in between those scenes in the porn you've seen, including showers, loads of hand washing and even sometimes sandwich breaks – they just don't show you those parts on the video.

Ask questions along the way, listen to what your partner says and let them take the lead. Again, just because you may be on top does not mean you should be the one in charge.

A SPECIAL NOTE ABOUT LUBRICATION

During vaginal sex, females produce natural lubricant fluids, which make penetration easier. The amount and effectiveness of each woman's natural lubrication varies throughout their lifetime, and their monthly cycle.

Anuses are not self-lubricating and anal sex without the addition of a lubricant can be very painful, it also greatly increases the risk of damage to the lining of the rectum as well as condom breakage. Some lubes are specifically designed for anal sex… look for water-based lubes with just a touch of silicone.

THERE ARE FOUR MAIN GROUPS OF LUBRICATION.

Glycerin lubes

Are water-based lubes, which means that they can be washed off with water, and when they dry out (as they sometimes do) can be reconstituted with water as well.

Glycerin dries fast and absorbs into the skin so they need to be reapplied or reconstituted often. The sugars in glycerin can contribute to yeast infections in females and should not be used if you are diabetic or if your immune system is compromised.

Glycerin does not stain sheets or eat away at condoms, but glycerin is an ingredient in laxatives, so do not use it for anal sex

Silicone lubes

Are less sticky and longer lasting form of water-based lube, because the silicone prevents the lube from drying out.

Most lubricated condoms are lubricated with silicone.

Not all silicone lubes are condom safe, though most are – check for the "CE" label.

Silicone cleans up with soap and water.

Natural oils

Are, typically, plant or vegetable-based and safe to eat – which means they are safe to put inside your body, HOWEVER, they will destroy condoms.

These are best saved for massages and masturbation.

Petroleum-based lubes

Are also oil-based, though they are synthetic (man-made) and NOT digestible. They also cause irritation inside vaginas and anuses and destroy condoms (making the spread of disease easier) as well as lacking any antibacterial properties.

These include things like Vaseline, lotions or hair conditioners.

Other general guidelines for lubes:

- Anything with oil in it will destroy a condom.

- In general, avoid lubes with scent, comic pictures, silly phrases…

- Any lubrication that has the ingredients of Lidocane or Benzocaine should be avoided. These things are desensitizers, which reduce your body's ability to feel pain and increase the likelihood of damage and infection.

A SPECIAL NOTE ABOUT NONOXYNOL-9

In the last decade, there has been a growing body of evidence, which has shown that nonoxynol-9 should not be used for vaginal or anal sex.

Nonoxynol-9 can kill both sperm and HIV, but it also causes irritation to the internal vaginal and anal walls, making it easier for HIV (and other diseases) to be transmitted because of abrasions.

Because of this, many HIV, AIDS and gay and women's health organizations including the Centers for Disease Control and the World Health Organization, have called to discontinue the sale of condoms that contain nonoxynol-9.[60]

Unfortunately it is the most popular spermicide in America.

You may not want to give up the slight (anti-pregnancy) benefit during vaginal sex,

OR

you may not think that the benefit is big enough to risk the possible damage by irritation.

The choice is yours regarding vaginal sex, though Nonoxynol-9 should NOT be used for anal sex.

SECTION V – CHOICE MAKING/ DECISION MAKING

Chapter 21

REGARDING ABSTINENCE

When people speak of "safe sex" today, they are generally referring to abstinence.

Choosing to be abstinent from sex and sexual play with other people is the only sure method to avoid Sexually Transmitted Infections (STI's) and to prevent an unplanned pregnancy.

Although, monogamy (having sex with only one other person, within a committed long-term relationship with someone who has tested free of any STIs) is also generally considered to be safe sex, it can lead to pregnancy.

Masturbation (by yourself) can also be considered, by definition, safe sex.

There are many ways in which you can give and receive sexual pleasure without having sexual intercourse. Fondling, kissing and hugging can be a way of sharing and showing loving and sexual feelings for each other. For some people (and at some times) these kinds of activities can be more fulfilling than sexual intercourse.

Some people decide that they do not want to start having sex until they are in a significant or long-term relationship, some decide to wait for marriage, or college, or prom, or Friday…

The decision to abstain from sexual behavior can be either a long-term decision or a short-term one.

It is important to know and trust yourself to decide if something is not the right thing for you at a particular time. It is also important to understand that you will probably meet someone you want and feel ready to have sex with and you need to be prepared.

We are only abstinent until we decide not to be.

A SPECIAL NOTE ABOUT ABSTINENCE CONTRACTS

Research from four cycles of the National Survey of Family Growth, which studies information on sexual and marital behaviors, reports that almost all Americans have sex before marrying, according to non-marital sex research, this behavior is the norm in the U.S. and has been for the past fifty years. A recent study published in Public Health Reports, shows that by age twenty, 75% of Americans have had non-marital sex.

Most teens who vow to save themselves for marriage, do not. When people do make these vows, however, they sometimes make the mistake of not preparing themselves or educating themselves for when they do decide to engage in sexual contact. Thinking, "that-stuff-doesn't-apply-to-me," leads to higher risks for pregnancy and disease, because chances are eventually it will apply to you.

Will you be prepared?

Like swimming, driving or CPR, even if you're not doing it right now, it is very important to prepare yourself for when the moment arises.

A Harvard School of Public Health study in 2006, published in The American Journal of Public Health, found that teens that made virginity pledges were 52% more likely to break that vow within a year of making it.[61]

This means abstinence vows, statistically, break four times as often as condoms.[62]

If you decide what feels right for you is to wait until marriage... then don't wear a special bracelet, don't sign your name on a list, don't join a club...

Just wait.

Anyone practicing abstinence should also be educated on other methods and have a backup!

All those other things do (the vows, the rings, the pins, the clubs) is make you think about sex – more specifically, the sex you are not having.

This is "The Cheesecake Rule". If you joined a club about NOT eating cheesecake and wore a bracelet on your wrist or a ring on your finger reminding you constantly to NOT eat cheesecake, would that really help you stay away? Or would it make you hungrier?

See, you're probably thinking about cheesecake right now.

By the way, just like no one should force, coerce or manipulate you into having sex, no one should be making you choose to not have sex, either.

Abstinence, like indulgence, is a choice. When/ if you choose to be abstinent, strive to make sure you are doing it for your own reasons and not someone else's. Part of growing up is learning what (and who, and when) is right for you.

The decision whether or not to remain abstinent should not be something that one has to feel ashamed of making or of breaking. Do not let someone intimidate, guilt, force or otherwise manipulate you into making any decision about your own body – whether that decision is to have sex or the decision is to not have sex. What you do with your own genitals is no one's choice but yours.

Chapter 22

SELF-ESTEEM

Self-esteem is the way we feel about ourselves. Issues with valuing ourselves enough can interfere with good decision-making.

- If you need others to fill gaps in your self esteem.

- If your self-image depends on what others think of you.

Or

- If you think you need to behave in certain ways to earn or keep someone else's love.

- This will put you in a position in which you may make choices that are not good for you.

The first time one has sex should be notable, and can be fun, exciting and pleasurable, but it can also be awkward and even painful.

Boys tend to be excited about puberty and look forward to sex. The changes in our bodies feel powerful and fun.

Girls on the other hand, sometimes have a harder time with puberty. The changes in their bodies can make them self-conscious, anxious and physically sore. Fewer girls report looking forward to sex the same way boys tend to.

Many people engage in sex for the first time because they confuse sex with love. They worry that others (including their partner) will think poorly of them if they do not have sex or like them more if they do.

If you have high self-esteem, you are more likely to make decisions that are safe and right for you.

Making decisions that are safe and right for you increases your self-esteem.

Some ways to improve your self-esteem are:

- Associating with people who genuinely care about you.
- Learning how to give and take compliments.
- Avoiding perfectionism.
- Improving your trouble areas.
- Setting goals and meeting them.
- Exercising.
- Getting involved in social activities.
- Focusing on things you already know you do well.
- Helping others.
- Remembering that everybody is different.

Chapter 23

REGARDING INDULGENCE

The decision whether or not to remain abstinent should not be something that one has to feel ashamed of doing or of not-doing.

Do not let anyone intimidate, guilt, force or otherwise manipulate you into making any decision about your own body – whether your decision is to have sex or your decision is to not have sex.

What you do with your own genitals is no one's choice but yours.

Thinking through all the implications of having sex can be a useful way of helping you arrive at a decision. For all the reasons there are to not have sex, there are just as many reasons why people choose to have sex.

Generational differences, political issues, spirituality and media also affect how and when people decide to express themselves sexually. Other things that can influence this decision include our own internal sense of responsibility and power, our relationships with ourselves and our bodies and knowledge about sex.

There is nothing wrong with making yourself feel good or enjoying making someone else feel good as long as:

- You are comfortable with what you are doing.

- You are doing it safely.

- You are doing it legally.

- You are aware of the consequences.

and

- No one (including yourself) is getting hurt.

Chapter 24

THINGS TO CONSIDER

Before choosing to engage in sex, there are questions to consider, such as:

- Does this feel right?

- Do I know what I am doing?

- Do I know what I want to be doing?

- Do I know the consequences?

- What would I do if I became pregnant?

- Does this compromise my relationship with myself?

- Does this compromise my relationship with my family

- Does this compromise my relationship with my connection to my spirituality?

- Do I want to wait until I am married?

- Do I need to be in a relationship to have sex?

- Do I need to have sex to be in a relationship?

- How do I define "sex"?

- How do I define "virginity"?

Another important thing to consider is how your partner answers these same questions.

All of these things can (and will) change as you get older and the world changes around you.

And just like changing your order while you were still holding a menu in your hands — some of our decisions can change in a matter of moments.

For now:

- Get clear about your wants needs as well as your limits, boundaries, desires and values.

- Know that these may be different than your friends' family's or partners'.

- Be solid with your choices so you can maintain them when faced with compromising situations or a changing landscape.

Speaking of compromising situations:

Alcohol and drugs will interfere with good choices, because substances disinhibit you — that means they allow you to make different choices than you would if you were thinking clearly.

Things to remember:

- If you can't talk about it you shouldn't be doing it.

- If you don't feel safe you shouldn't be doing it.

- What is safe and mature may not always be what feels best.

- What feels best may not always be safe or mature.

Chapter 25

VIRGINITY

Virginity is like a candle, not a light bulb.

It diminishes with time and experience, it is not turned off or on like it is connected to a switch.

It is also not something one "gives" to or "takes" from another person.

What defines you as a sexual person or gives you value as a partner should not be defined by what you have done or not done up to that point.

Over-emphasizing one specific act at one specific time, can lead people to engage in acts that they do not like, or are not right for them.

Every new experience and partner can be important, game-changing, and can bring feelings (both physical and emotional) that you have not felt before.

A SPECIAL NOTE ABOUT SIGNS

Signs You Should Keep Communicating

- You both come to a mutual decision about how far to go.
- You both clearly express comfort with the situation.
- You both have been clear about what you want and what you don't want.
- You both feel comfortable and safe stopping at any time.
- Consent has clearly been given.
- You both are excited and having fun.

Signs You Should Pause and Talk

- You are not sure what the other person wants.
- You feel like you are getting mixed signals.
- You have not talked about what you want to do.
- You assume that you will do the same thing as before.
- Your partner stops or is not responsive.

Signs You Should Stop

- You are too intoxicated to gauge or give consent.
- Your partner is asleep or passed out.
- You hope your partner will say nothing and go with the flow.
- You intend to have sex by any means necessary.
- You haven't or don't plan to tell your friends or family about your partner or your level of sexual activity.
- You don't know your partner.

PART FOUR: RISK REDUCTION

SECTION VI – RISK REDUCTION

Chapter 26

*SEXUALLY TRANSMITTED INFECTIONS
(STI'S)*

Currently, there are more than a dozen separate organisms and syndromes classified as Sexually Transmitted Infections.[63]

Infections that spread through sexual contact and activity have been known by several names. "Social diseases," "Venereal Disease (VD)" and "STDs" (for Sexually Transmitted Diseases). Most recently, though, the trend has turned toward referring to them as STI's for Sexually Transmitted Infections.

The main driving force behind this is that the word "disease" implies an obvious, medical problem – complete with signs and symptoms. Because many of these "social diseases" are caused by bacteria or viruses, which do not necessarily have clear signs and/or may have symptoms that can go unnoticed for long periods of times, the term "infection" is more accurate.

Several of these, including HPV, HIV, and Chlamydia, can have long-term health ramifications including infertility, cancer and death while exhibiting hardly any symptoms.

More than eighteen million Americans contract an STI each year.[64]

Nine million of them are teenagers (ages fifteen to twenty-five).[65]

There are ten thousand new diagnoses every day.

(This averages out to one every eight seconds).[66]

The CDC estimates that half of all young adults in the U.S. will contract a sexually transmitted infection by age twenty-five.[67]

If you think or worry or know that you have been exposed to any STI,

- Don't panic.

- Don't ignore it.

- Get checked out and treated by a doctor as soon as possible. Taking a friend, partner or supportive adult with you is also a good idea. There, you will get helpful info, a decrease in your stress level, probably a bit of tough love and some medication, if you need it.

- And don't have sex again until you do.

Sexually transmitted infections happen. There is no 100% safe sex just as there is no 100% safe salad bars or 100% safe drivers.

If you do get an infection (and many of you will), do your best to not let it affect your self-esteem – if you are doing due diligence and are responsibly taking precautions – contracting an infection does not make you a bad person any more than food poisoning or fender benders do.

Chapter 27

STI PRIMER

STI's are grouped into categories

Bacterial

- Vaginitis / Urethritis
- Chancroid
- Gonorrhea
- Chlamydia
- Syphilis
- PID

Fungal

- Mycoses
- (Jock itch)
- (Yeast infection)

Parasites

- Crabs

- Trichomoniasis

Viral

This class of STI's is systemic and includes viral infections that affect organ systems other than just the reproductive system. There are no known cures for these viruses, though currently there are vaccines for at least two…

These are the scariest – The four H's

- Herpes

- Hepatitis B

- HPV (Human Papilloma Virus)

- HIV/AIDS

BACTERIAL STI'S

Vaginitis / Urethritis

These inflammations are very common and caused by small amounts of bacteria or yeast in the vagina or urethra, which grow more than normal. Persons with either of these conditions (Vaginitis for females/ Urethritis in males) may also have itching or burning of the genital area, foul odors and discharge and pain while urinating or having sex.

Bacterial STI's usually cause a watery, white, cottage cheese-like discharge, which is itchy and irritating to the vagina and the surrounding skin. Urethritis can include dysuria (pain or a burning sensation upon urination), a white/cloudy discharge and a feeling that one needs to pee almost constantly.

Condoms offer very good protection, but both partners can be successfully treated with oral or topical antibiotics and/or antifungal creams.

Scary Fact:

When passed sexually, these are usually caused by an infectious organism – such as Chlamydia or Gonorrhea. If left untreated, these can reach the fallopian tubes and ovaries (or epydidymis in men) and could lead to infertility.

Chancroid

This especially dangerous sexually transmitted bacterium appears in the form of a small, pus filled, and painful ulcer on the genitals. Women do not get sores but do get painful urination, intercourse and vaginal discharge and pain when they pee. Men also develop buboes-when the lymph glands in the groin become swollen.

Chancroid can be prevented with condoms, and treated with oral antibiotics.

Scary Fact:

Chancroid sores increase the chances of getting HIV.

Gonorrhea

This microscopic parasite spread via vaginal, anal, and oral intercourse. Gonorrhea is a bacterium, which causes sterility, arthritis, and heart problems, and a pus-like discharge from the urethra, which causes pain during urination.

Condoms offer very good protection against Gonorrhea, but both partners can be successfully treated with oral antibiotics. Often people with gonorrhea also have Chlamydia and must be treated for both infections at the same time.

Scary Fact:

Gonorrhea is one of the most common and the most invisible STIs. 80% of the women and 10% of the men with Gonorrhea show no symptoms[68], but continue to pass on more than 700,000 new cases of Gonorrhea every year.[69]

Chlamydia

This sneaky bacterium has few symptoms in the beginning, but will cause painful and burning discharges during urination and intercourse, inflammation of the rectum and cervix, swelling of the testicles, bleeding after sex and, eventually, sterility. It is spread through vaginal and anal intercourse and there have been cases of passing the parasite from the hand to the eye.

Chlamydia is easily prevented with condoms and (if caught early enough) treated with antibiotics for a week. Chlamydia can be misdiagnosed and confused with Gonorrhea.

Scary Fact:

Most women and half of the men who have this disease do not know that they have it and are still spreading the disease. Three million American men and women become affected every year.[70]

Syphilis

This organism (called "spirochete") is sexually transmitted, causes a series of phases (in no particular order), which often overlap and have their own, distinctive sets of symptoms.

The first phase starts with painless, crater-like sores in your swimsuit area or around your mouth, which ooze a highly infectious liquid.

Without antibiotics, a month later, a painful rash on your palms and the soles of your feet appear.

The third phase has no symptoms and can last for years, which (although it sounds nice) is highly unfortunate because, if left untreated, the last phase kicks in involving hair loss, brain damage, physical disfigurement, paralysis and death.

Condom use and antibiotics are your only defense against spirochete. Damage done during the late stages cannot be undone.

Scary Fact:

Some people don't think that syphilis still exists.

Pelvic Inflammatory Disease

PID is a serious infection, which develops when an infection spreads up from the vagina and cervix into the reproductive organs. PID is usually the result of a sexually transmitted infection such as Chlamydia or Gonorrhea. They are spread by vaginal and anal intercourse and, sometimes, oral sex. More than one million women are diagnosed each year.[71] If PID is not treated, it can cause serious problems, such as infertility, ectopic pregnancy, and chronic pain.

Condoms offer very good protection against PID. A health care provider can diagnose Pelvic Inflammatory Disease during a pelvic exam. Tests will also be done for Chlamydia, Gonorrhea, or other infections, because they often cause PID. PID is treated most often with antibiotics and a period of bed rest and abstinence.

Scary Fact:

In more developed cases of PID, surgery may be needed to repair or remove reproductive organs.

FUNGAL STI'S

Jock Itch

Tinea Cruris is the scientific name a fungal infection of the (usually male) groin region, commonly called "Jock Itch."

This infection is usually caused by a warm, damp environment which allows the fungus to grow out of control – such as tight, sweaty or rubbing clothing (such as a jockstrap). Fungus from other parts of the body (like Tinea Pedis or "Athlete's Foot'") can also contribute to Jock Itch. It causes itching or a burning sensation in the genital and surrounding areas. Affected areas may appear red or brown, with flaking, peeling or cracking skin. Mycosis infections are commonly treated with antimycotics (antifungal drugs) and steroids.

Indirect transmission may also occur as the fungi can survive in bed linens, towels and articles of clothing for long periods of time.

To help prevent these types of infections, do not share unwashed towels, clothing (especially underwear) or bed linens that have not been washed. As always, good hygiene is a good thing – as is anything that keeps these areas clean and dry, such as bathing regularly and wearing cotton, non-occlusive underwear (this means boxer briefs, boys), which is changed every day.

Scary Fact:

Men can also contract yeast infections in their urethras as well as Urinary Tract Infections (UTI's). UTI's are caused by bacteria infecting the urethra (rather than yeast).[72] If you think you might have a UTI, go see a doctor, because the infection can travel up past the bladder, causing kidney damage.

Yeast Infection

Candidiasis (commonly called a yeast infection or thrush) is a fungal infection of the vagina.

Candida yeasts are usually present in most women, but are kept in check by other naturally occurring bacteria. However, external irritants (such as some detergents or douches, glycerin – based lubricants and intercourse with an unbathed partners) or internal disturbances (caused by things such as medications, contraceptives or pregnancy), can mess with the delicate pH balance of the vagina, and an overgrowth of yeast can result.

Most medical descriptions compare the discharge to ricotta cheese and the scent of baked bread. There is an intense itching, burning sensation, localized in the vagina and vulva, which can become so painful it can become hard to walk. Mycosis infections are commonly treated with antimycotics (antifungal drugs) and steroids.

Yeast can be transmitted between people by direct contact, and so can be considered a sexually transmitted infection. A yeast-infected person can infect other partners, then get re-infected the next time they have sex with them. Indirect transmission may also occur as the fungi can survive in bed linens, towels and articles of clothing for long periods of time.

To help prevent these types of infections, do not share unwashed towels, clothing (especially underwear) and keep your sheets clean. As always, good hygiene is a good thing as is anything that keeps these areas clean and dry, such as bathing regularly and wearing cotton, non-occlusive underwear, which is changed every day.

Scary Fact:

There are other nasty creatures besides yeast that can infect your crotch. Urinary Tract Infections, or UTI's, are due to bacteria infecting the urethra rather than yeast. If you think you might have a UTI, go see a doctor, because the infection can travel up past the bladder, causing kidney damage.

PARASITIC STI'S

Crabs

Also called "pubic lice", "scabies" and "cooties", this is an easily transferred STI that not even condoms help with – and they're bugs. Tiny, grey bugs that attach to your skin, turn darker when swollen with blood, and attach eggs to your pubic hair. They resemble crabs, live off of your blood supply and make you itch like a crazy person.

Treatment consists of a couple of doses of special lice shampoos. The dead crabs (and their eggs) have to be pulled out of your pubes with a tiny comb.

Wash clothes, bed sheets etc. with hot, hot, hot water and some of the shampoo. The only protection against this infection is to limit your number of intimate and sexual contacts and avoid people who don't. Other things that help prevent this include, washing clothes from used clothing stores, avoiding people who can't stop scratching their crotches, and not sleeping in sheets that do not seem clean – especially if they are in beds of people you don't know very well.

Scary Fact:
Scabies is a similar bug, but they burrow under your skin instead of clinging to the hair.

Trichomoniasis

Trichomoniasis is caused by the single-celled protozoan parasite, Trichomoniasis Vaginalis. The vagina is the most common site of infection, though the urethra in men can also be affected.

Most guys with Trich do not have signs or symptoms – however, some guys feel irritation inside the penis, discharge with a strong odor, or a slight burning after urination and ejaculation.

Symptoms usually appear within one to three weeks of exposure, but the parasite is harder to detect in men than in women.

When someone has been infected, both partners should be treated at the same time to eliminate the parasite. People should avoid sex until both partners finish treatment and have no symptoms. Latex male condoms, when used consistently and correctly, can reduce the risk of transmission.

Scary Fact:

An infected person (even if they have never had symptoms or the symptoms have stopped) can continue to infect or re-infect other partners until he has been treated.

VIRAL STI'S

Herpes

There are two forms of this virus: simplex 1 and simplex 2. The first one is associated with cold sores or fever blisters. The second involves hot, itchy blisters, which burst open and create ulcers.

Both can be transmitted sexually, and start out with flu-like symptoms followed by a recurring rash which includes clusters of the tingly sores (simplex 1 on the mouth, simplex 2 "down there", "back there", "under there" and everywhere in between). Once infected, symptoms can be triggered by stress, and include painful burning during urination.

Herpes is most contagious from the time sores are present until the scabs fall off, but some people can be contagious even when they do not have symptoms. Mucous membranes of the mouth, anus, vagina, penis, and the eyes are especially susceptible to infection. One million new cases are diagnosed every year.[73]

Condoms help to prevent herpes, but only when the sores are not already present. Medications can decrease the number and intensity of outbreaks, but Herpes is not curable, and like many other viruses, remains with you for life. Don't touch anybody anywhere with any part of you that has sores until they heal, wash your hands often and do not touch the sores.

Scary Fact:

Sores may be spread from one partner to another or one part of the body to another, whenever contact is made.

Hepatitis B

This virus is transmitted sexually and through all bodily fluids, is very sneaky and very, very, very contagious. In the beginning it causes extreme fatigue, headache, fever and vomiting. Later on, symptoms include yellow skin, brown urine and attacks on the liver, which lead to cirrhosis, cancer and possibly death. Almost 40,000 Americans get HVB every year (and an estimated 1.2 million people in the us have it right now).[74]

Condoms offer some protection against HVB during vaginal, anal, and oral intercourse, but the virus can be passed through kissing and other intimate touching. In some cases, the infection clears up in a couple of months, but some people remain contagious for the rest of their lives. This STI is preventable with a vaccine – but only if you get it ahead of time. If you were born before 1991 and/or did not get it as an infant, go get it. Now.

Scary Fact:

Hepatitis is over 100% more contagious than HIV.[75]

HPV (Genital Warts)

There are approximately ninety different kinds of these cell-mutating Human Papilloma Viruses that cause a variety of itchy, flesh-colored, cauliflower-like warts. Also called HPV, this disease is spread through genital contact with or without symptoms. There are a few strains of HPV that do not manifest in warts, but these ones can cause cancers in the cervix, vulva and penis.

Genital warts can be prevented with condoms, and treated with suppression medications, professional freezing, topical creams lasers and acids in places you really don't want lasers and acids. A vaccine has been developed (go ask your doctor!), but at this time there is no cure. Rumor has it that after several years you can "grow out of it", but this has not been proven.

Scary Fact:

If left untreated, the warts can grow to block the openings of the vagina, anus, urethra or throat.

HIV (Human Immunodeficiency Virus)

This viral infection can weaken the body's ability to fight disease and cause acquired immune deficiency syndrome (AIDS) – the last stage of HIV infection. HIV is spread in blood, semen and vaginal fluids. HIV remains in the body for life and is the most dangerous of all STI's, causing weight loss, constant uncomfortable diarrhea, purplish growths on the skin, pneumonia, a variety of cancers and death.

HIV is prevented through condom use and can be managed by drugs. It is incurable, currently fatal and, at this time, no one has recovered.

Scary Fact:

There may be no symptoms for ten or more years.

Chapter 28

HIV/AIDS 101

HIV stands for the Human Immunodeficiency Virus – a virus which can infect and live in your body, which slowly weakens your immune system – our body's mechanism for fighting off infections.

Specifically, HIV attacks a type of white blood cell called the T lymphocyte (or T cell). T cells are one specific type of blood cell that helps defend against infections and diseases.

If HIV enters the body, it attacks a T cell and slowly works its way inside the cell. Once inside, the virus takes over and uses the cell as a virus-making factory to copy itself. The newly made viruses then leave the T cell and go on to infect and destroy other T cells. This is how it multiplies. Once a T cell has been invaded, they can no longer fight illnesses within the body.

The T-cell range in the typical human is between 500-1800 (typically 800-1200).

When a person's T-cell count drops below 200 their immune system is considered compromised (too weak to keep us safe from infections), this is called AIDS. Acquired Immune Deficiency Syndrome.

AIDS makes us very susceptible to other bacterial and viral infections that we would normally be able to fend off. AIDS doesn't kill you – AIDS makes you die from other things. Even things like the common cold, which are easily fought off by healthy immune systems, can become very dangerous.

Being infected with HIV and having AIDS are different things.

Someone who is infected with HIV is called HIV-Positive. Being HIV-Positive does not mean that someone will progress to full-blown AIDS. Some people can stay relatively healthy and symptom free for several years – even longer with medications that are available today. The term "Poz" has been embraced, particularly in the gay community, for people who are HIV-Positive.

People are diagnosed with AIDS when they have a very low number of active T cells left and show signs of a serious infection. There is a list of thirty-three AIDS-defining illnesses, called opportunistic infections, which take advantage of weakened immune systems.

20 years ago, AIDS meant that someone was dying. This is different today, thanks to medication regimes.

There is no cure for AIDS. Although there are medication regimes that can slow down its progress and researchers understand the virus more and more each year, AIDS is still considered fatal.

HIV is spread through blood, semen, vaginal secretions and breast milk. Transmission occurs when any of these four infected fluids move from one person's body into another's.

Infection can happen via:

- Unprotected sex with an infected partner

- Sharing needles during drug use

- Transmission of fluids from mothers to babies during childbirth or breastfeeding

People who have another sexually transmitted infection, such as Syphilis, Genital Herpes, Chlamydia or Gonorrhea are at greater risk for getting HIV during sex if they have an infected partner. Some STI's increase risk due to the presence of sores, but any infection in the body will trigger the immune system to attack with more and more T-cells, which the HIV virus feeds on.

Although the HIV-Positive person may look and feel healthy – the virus is silently reproducing itself destroying more and more T cells. It can take a while for someone's body to recognize it is under attack or show symptoms, which is a major factor in why the disease is still spreading.

Scary Fact:

Half of all HIV infections in the U.S. occur among persons under the age of twenty-five.[76]

It is possible to find HIV in the saliva, tears, sweat and urine of infected individuals, but there are no recorded cases of infection by these secretions. Animals and insects do not pass on the disease, nor can HIV be transmitted via sharing forks or spoons, water, food, toilet seats or even hot tubs and swimming pools with infected people.

The CDC reports use of latex (or polyurethane) condoms during vaginal, anal or oral intercourse significantly reduces the risk of HIV transmission.[77] The risk is lower for the penetrative partner than the receptive partner (in general). Though oral sex has relatively low risk due to the low PH levels in the mouth and enzymes in saliva, which kill HIV, any anal sex causes microscopic tearing and non-visible amounts of blood. There are also studies that have shown that HIV can penetrate healthy, intact, vaginal lining.

Intravenous drug users should not share needles or injection equipment.

Just as overactive immune systems increase risk of HIV infection, so do compromised ones, so self-care and stress management are important risk reduction tools as well.

Just because someone is exposed, does not mean that they will be infected.

Testing is important and best done within three months. 90-95% of infected people will have enough antibodies to show up in testing within the first twenty-five to thirty days after infection. By the three-month mark, most everyone will.

After that three-month mark, HIV rapid tests can be taken at public health clinics, results can be obtained in as quickly as twenty minutes. There are two tests – the first is the ELISA test, which screens for antibodies.

A negative ELISA test means you are HIV-Negative.

A positive ELISA test means you need to take a second test – a western blot test, which screens for the virus itself.

A person needs a positive response to at least one of these tests to be diagnosed HIV-Positive.

In terms of medication, after exposure there are post-exposure Prophylaxes, a month-long medication regimen, which greatly decreases the likelihood of infection – especially if taken within twenty-four to seventy-two hours of infection. This is usually acquired in emergency rooms and works by stopping the infection before it reaches the lymph nodes.

The medications are extremely hard on the body and quite expensive $800-2000 for the month's supply.

There are pre-exposure prophylaxes in the works as well.[78]

A SPECIAL NOTE ABOUT VACCINES

Two of the most serious STIs now have vaccines available.

The first is Hepatitis B.

Depending on which of two different vaccines your medical provider carries, a series of two or three shots over a six month is given to teens or preteens between the ages of eleven and eighteen. It has been part of the recommended immunization schedule for babies born after 1991 in the U.S.[79]

It is important to find out if you have received the vaccines because, though HVB is generally considered an adult disease, it is extremely contagious and teens get infected as well. Thanks to the immunization, HVB infections have dropped 95% since routine immunization began in the early 1990s,[80] though the Centers for Disease Control estimates that approximately a million people in America carry HVB in their blood and 5000 people a year die from this virus.[81]

The second is HPV.

There is now a vaccine that prevents the types of genital Human Papilloma Viruses (HPV), which cause most cases of cervical cancer and genital warts. The vaccine, Gardasil, is given in three shots over six-months. The vaccine is routinely recommended for people of ages nine through twenty-six who have not yet been vaccinated, especially if they are sexually active.[82]

It is theoretically possible that if every young woman can become vaccinated once she becomes sexually active, that cervical cancer may be eliminated completely in future generations.

Do not be fooled by the assumption that HPV is a girl-thing because the vaccine is pushed for teen girls and associated with cervical cancer.

A 2011 study from the Cancer Center and Research Institute, reported that half of all American men might be infected with the Human Papilloma Virus.[83]

The HPV vaccines are approved for guys (9-26) as well, and along with condoms is one of your two biggest weapons against HPV.

Our third weapon against it is our immune systems, which clear most HPV infections with little difficulty or problem, however the strain, HPV-16 is connected to the mouth, throat, head, neck and anal cancers IN MEN. HPV can be spread through oral and anal sex as well as vaginal sex.

You can guarantee that if and when you choose to become sexually active, you will be exposed to some strain of the almost 100 different types of HPV (Genital Warts being one of them). Vaccinating males will have health benefits for them by preventing genital warts and rare cancers, such as penile and anal cancer. It is also possible that vaccinating boys/men will have indirect health benefits for girls/women.

There are currently no screening processes for men to help doctors find out if you have it.

This means guys do not usually know they have it until a lesion appears somewhere on their body.

HPV is a boy issue as well – get vaccinated.[84]

Chapter 29

CONTRACEPTION/SAFER SEX

Techniques have been developed to reduce the chances of conception. Culture and law have both developed slower than this technology, leading to controversy about moral, ethical, and legal grounds for the use of contraception and safer sex.

Contraceptives reduce the likelihood of pregnancy.

Safer Sex deals with the reduction of exposure to disease.

All sexually active people can benefit from proper and consistent uses of both contraceptives and safer sex practices.

If you are sexually active and not using some form of contraception, you have a 90% chance of getting (or getting someone) pregnant in the next year.[87]

These techniques are not always easy to use or do.

They can be hard to talk about, to learn or to remember.

They can be complicated, messy, inconvenient, awkward and not 100% effective, even when done properly.

No contraceptive is 100% effective – even abstinence.

Abstinence is not 100% effective because:

- People may change their mind and may not have taken the time to educate themselves on other methods.

- People will have sex eventually and may not have taken the time to educate themselves on other methods.

- People can be pressured or forced into having sex.

Feeling safe that you and your partner are doing everything you can to be safe and protected makes sexual behavior less stressful and more exciting.

When choosing the method that works best for you:

The method needs to

- Be effective (to avoid pregnancy and disease). Failure rates for safer sex and contraceptive methods are defined as the likelihood of failure in the first year of using.

- Be safe (to avoid medical consequences).

- Fit your personal lifestyle (to avoid being forgotten or used inconsistently).

- Do the same things for your partner (for all of the above reasons).

An important point to remember is to avoid placing all of the responsibility for protection on the other person. Safer sex is the responsibility of both partners. The stress, responsibility, the time involved as well as the money should be shared – just like the babies or the bugs would be.

Chapter 30

THE PROCESS OF CONTRACEPTION

The separation of intercourse from pregnancy uses methods that stop one of the three stages of reproduction:

Release and Transport of gametes (sperm and egg).

Fertilization – The fusion of the sperm and egg.

This usually occurs in the upper third of the fallopian tubes/oviduct. Thirty minutes after ejaculation, sperm are present in the oviduct, having swam from the vagina through the uterus and into the tubes. Of the several hundred million sperm released in the ejaculation, only a few thousand reach the egg.

Of those few thousand, only one sperm will fertilize the egg. One sperm fuses with receptors on the surface of the egg, triggering a series of chemical changes in the outer membrane that prevent any other sperm from entering the egg. Fusion of the egg and sperm form what is called a zygote.

Implantation – The uterine lining becomes enlarged and prepared for implantation of the embryo.

The lining of the uterus and the embryo interlock to form the placenta, the nourishing boundary between the mother's and embryo's systems. The umbilical cord extends from the placenta to the embryo, and transports food to and wastes from the embryo.

Chapter 31

CONTRACEPTIVE/SAFER SEX METHODS

Contraceptive/Safer Sex methods can be grouped into the following five categories:

NATURAL METHODS (which use few, if any, additional devices and rely mostly on cooperation and timing)

ABSTINENCE

Abstinence is choosing not to participate in sexual behavior with other people.

Positives:

- No side effects
- Abstinence is accepted by most religions

Negatives:

- Refraining is difficult to do for some people
- Abstinence eventually ends for most people

Abstinence can be considered approximately 75% effective (because approximately a quarter of teens who practice abstinence become pregnant within one year).[85]

Anyone practicing abstinence should be educated on other methods as well and have a back-up plan.

ALTERNATIVES

Alternative methods involve the penetration of orifices other than the vagina – such as the mouth and anus.

Positives:

- Can be incorporated into sex play
- Low risk of pregnancy (unless sperm accidentally lands on woman's vulva)

Negatives:

- Alternative penetration does not prevent the spread of disease

Alternatives can be considered 99% effective.[89]

MASTURBATION

Masturbation is sexually pleasing oneself (or another) using manual techniques, instrumental manipulation, fantasy or combinations of these.

Positives:

- Costs nothing
- Can be done quickly and conveniently
- Reduces stress
- Can be incorporated into sex play

Negatives:

- Masturbation is frowned upon by some religions

Masturbation can be considered 100% effective.

RHYTHM METHODS

Rhythm methods are also called Fertility awareness methods (or FAM's). These methods involve the charting of the menstrual cycles in order to predict approximately nine "unsafe" days in which one does not have intercourse by checking temperature/ urine/ calendars or changes in cervical mucus.

Positives:

- No side effects

- Calendars, thermometers and charts are easy to get.

- FAM's are accepted by most religions

Negatives:

- They rhythm method requires frequent monitoring

- Irregular periods, mucus or temperature changes can make estimation difficult.

Rhythm methods can be considered 75% effective.[86]

SPERMICIDES
(WHICH KILL SPERM)

SPERMICIDE

Spermicide can be a foam, cream, jelly, film suppository or tablet placed inside the vagina, which kills and blocks sperm from entering the vaginal canal.

Positives:

- Spermicide is effective immediately after insertion

- No hormones are involved

- Adds lubrication

Negatives:

- Requires a clinician visit

- Requires practice

- Spermicide can irritate membranes

- Spermicide can be messy

- Spermicide can have an unpleasant taste

- Spermicide can be cumbersome to carry

Spermicide can be considered 75% effective.[87]

SPONGE

Sponges are soft, disc-shaped devices made of polyurethane foam, which contain spermicide. Once moistened to activate the spermicide, the sponge is placed inside the vagina to cover the cervix and prevent pregnancy and fitted with a small loop for easy removal and disposal.

Positives:

- Convenient

- Effective for more than one act of intercourse

- Effective for up to twenty-four hours

Negatives:

- Risk of toxic shock syndrome if left in for more than thirty hours

Sponges can be considered 78-85% effective.[88]

BARRIER METHODS (which prevent the fertilization of a woman's egg by blocking sperm)

BARRIERS
(CERVICAL CAP/ DIAPHRAGM/ SHIELD)

Barriers come in a few forms; a custom-fitted thimble-shaped latex cap (cervical cap), shallow rubber cup (diaphragm) or a silicone cup attached to the cervix via suction (shield). These cover the cervix, to prevent the passage of sperm and are sometimes filled with spermicide.

Positives:

- Barriers are reusable and can last several years

- Barriers can be left in place for up to forty-eight hours (they require additional spermicide before repeated intercourse)

Negatives:

- Some people are allergic to latex

- Barriers cannot be used during menstruation

- Barriers can be messy due to the necessity of spermicide

- There is a possible increase of bladder infections

Cervical barriers can be considered 78-85% effective.[89]

DENTAL DAMS

Dams are ultra-thin, often scented, latex sheets ranging from 6"x6" to 8"x12" (condoms cut up the side and unrolled can also be used), and placed over the vulva or anus during oral sex.

Positives:

- Convenient

- Inexpensive

Negatives:

- Dams create less sensitivity

Dams can be considered 85-97% effective.[90]

MALE CONDOMS

Condoms are latex coverings placed on the penis to prevent sperm from entering the vagina, anus or mouth.

Positives:

- Easy to find/ purchase
- Condoms helps reduce premature ejaculation
- Condoms can be incorporated into sex play

Negatives:

- Some people are allergic to latex
- Condoms can create a loss of sensation
- Condoms are less effective when used without hormonal methods

Condoms can be considered 78-85% effective.[91]

FEMALE CONDOMS

Female condoms are longer, wider form of male condoms, inserted into the vagina or rectum and held in place with bendable rings at both ends.

They are not called female condoms because they are "for girls," they are called female condoms because they go on the inside.

Positives:

- Female condoms are easy to find/ purchase
- Female condoms can be used as part of sex play

- Erection are unnecessary to keep in place

- Female condoms will not cause latex allergies

Negatives:

- Sometimes noisy or irritating

- The outer ring can be accidentally pushed inside

Female condoms can be considered 78-85% effective.[92]

OUTERCOURSE

Outercourse is sex with clothes on and/or that avoids penetration of any kind, also called "dry sex" or "dry humping."

Positives:

- No side effects

- No preparation necessary

- Outercourse may enhance orgasm later

Negatives:

- Outercourse relies on self-control and is difficult for some people to do.

- Pregnancy can still occur if any sperm land on a woman's vulva

- Dry sex does not prevent against disease when clothing is removed

Outercourse can be considered 99% effective.[98]

HORMONAL METHODS (which stop ovulation and prevent the possibility of fertilization; which thicken the woman's cervical mucus, making penetration of the uterus by sperm more difficult; or which alter the lining of the uterus so that the fertilized egg has difficulty implanting).

THE PILL

A birth control pill is a daily pill of progestin and/ or estrogen hormones, which is taken once a day. Both kinds of pill help thicken cervical mucus (preventing sperm from getting through) and prevent fertilized eggs from implanting in the uterus. The combination pill also prevents the eggs from releasing. Seasonale, A ninety-one-day regimen (Twelve weeks of active pills followed by one week of inactive pills) is also available which reduces periods to approximately four per year.

Positives:

- Periods become more regular and less severe

Negatives:

- Pills must be taken daily

- Side effects such as weight changes, depression, nausea and breast tenderness as well as other health risks.

- Health risks increase for smokers or those who are overweight

The Pill can be considered 91-98% effective.[93]

THE PATCH

Ortho-Evra is a slow-releasing hormonal patch, placed on a woman's body (anywhere but the breast), which prevents fertilization and implantation of eggs. The Patch is worn everyday and changed weekly (with the exception of one week per month in which no patch is necessary).

Positives:

- Convenient

Negatives:

- Patches may move, accidentally be removed or be unsightly.

The Patch can be considered 91-98% effective.[94]

THE SHOT

There are two types of hormonal birth control shots, which prevent the releasing and joining of eggs as well as the implantation of fertilized eggs. Shots are given either once per month (Lunelle) or every three months (Depo-Provera).

Positives:

- Can be effective up to three months
- Reduces cramps
- Convenient

Negatives:

- Side effects can include irregular bleeding, headaches, emotional changes
- It can take up to the three months to reverse the effects.

The shot can be considered 91-98% effective.[101]

THE VAGINAL RING

The NuvaRing is a combination of the pill and cervical cap in the form of a bendable, two-inch plastic ring (NuvaRing) worn around the cervix for three weeks each month.

Positives:

- Discreet
- Convenient
- Placement does not need to be exact

Negatives:

- The ring can cause vaginal irritation and discharge
- Physical risks include can worsen diabetes and high blood pressure and increased risk for heart attack and stroke.

- If ring is remains out for more than three hours, another birth control method must be used until the ring has been used continuously for seven days.

The Vaginal Ring can be considered 91-98% effective.[96]

IUD/IUS

Intrauterine instruments are small, plastic, T-shaped device inserted into the woman's uterus containing either copper (also known as an Intrauterine Device) or hormones (also known as Intrauterine System or Mirena) both of which help prevent the fertilization and implantation of eggs.

Positives:

- Can be left in for one (hormonal) to twelve (copper) years

- Helps reduce cramping (hormonal).

- The non-hormonal IUS is the only method available with as high a success rate as birth control pills.

Negatives:

- Cramps can be increased with the copper form

- Heavier and longer periods

Intrauterine instruments can be considered 99% effective.[97]

THE IMPLANT

Implanon is a small, plastic rod inserted under the skin of a woman's arm, releasing progestin, which help prevent the fertilization and implantation of eggs.

Positives:

- Can be left in for up to three years.

- The ability to become pregnant returns relatively quickly after removal.

Negatives:

- Slight scarring

- Irregular and unpredictable menstrual periods

- Certain medications (and possibly being overweight) can make the implant less effective.

Implanon can be considered 99% effective.[98]

ECP's

"Emergency Contraceptive Pills are also called "Plan B". These are two increased doses of estrogen and progestin taken twelve hours apart and within seventy-two hours to thicken mucus and prevent the releasing of eggs.

They are used by some as a back-up when other means of contraception have failed – for example, if a woman has forgotten to take a birth control pill or when a condom is torn during sex. It is also a first line of treatment for victims of sexual assault.

The phrase "morning-after pill" is a misnomer that is falling out of use due to the fact they are licensed for use up to seventy-two hours after sexual intercourse. Emergency contraception or "emergency contraceptive pills" is the phrase preferred by the medical community.

Unlike forms of chemical abortion such as Mifepristone, emergency contraception does not end pregnancies and will not harm a developing embryo.

ECP's are not to be confused with chemical abortion drugs like Mifepristone (formerly RU-486) also called Mifeprex, that act after implantation has occurred. RU-486 will induce abortion in the first forty-nine days (approximately nine weeks) of gestation using medication rather than surgery. It acts by blocking the hormone progesterone, which is essential to maintaining a pregnancy.

ECP's are not effective as an ongoing method of contraception. They also do not protect against sexually-transmitted infections.

If a woman takes the drug after the egg has already been released, it won't stave off fertilization or end a pregnancy. The pill must be taken before implantation, or it will have no effect. On day one, 95% of pregnancies are prevented, compared with 85% on the second day, and 60% for those starting on the third day.[99]

MEDICAL METHODS
(WHICH REQUIRE A DOCTOR'S INTERVENTION)

STERILIZATION

Surgical sterilization involves a doctor severing the tubes, which carry sperm in men (vasectomy) and the tubes in which the sperm and egg meet in women (tubal ligation). Small, (non-surgical) metallic implants called Essure, are also available for women. These are inserted into the fallopian tubes to block pregnancy by building-up scar tissue.

Positives:

- Permanent

- No lasting side effects

Negatives:

- Mild bleeding after surgery

- Sterilization is difficult to reverse

- Sterilization does not protect against disease.

Sterilization can be considered 99% effective.[100]

ABORTION

Abortion means ending the life of a developing fetus via a number of techniques. Although many abortions are used as birth control it is by no means a contraceptive and should be considered neither a mature nor responsible approach to sex.

Positives:

- Abortion can be used at times in which there are serious health concerns for the mother or fetus, in response to pregnancy arising from abuse or unwanted sex or in the event of ineffective or improperly used birth control

Negatives:

- Abortion can be both physically and psychologically damaging in possibly life-threatening ways.

Abortion can be considered 100% effective.[101]

Whether you abstain from sex or use some form of protection, it will take discipline, patience and the ability to delay gratification.

A SPECIAL NOTE ABOUT ABORTION

The national rates of unintended pregnancy and abortion rates have declined after contraceptive use went up starting in the 1980's. Though one million legal abortions are performed in America every year.[102]

There is more than one way an abortion is performed.

One is called **Vacuum Aspiration.** This is usually chosen if the pregnancy has been going on for less than twelve weeks. A thin tube is inserted through the cervix into the uterus and the contents are literally suctioned out.

If the pregnancy has gone past twelve weeks, (but no more than twenty-four weeks) a second method called **D&E** (Dilation and Evacuation) is possible. The cervix is opened (dilated) and a small, spoon-like instrument (a curette) is used to scrape the walls of the uterus, removing anything there, then suction is used to clear (evacuate) the uterus.

There is also a third method – **medicinal abortion** with a pill called Mifepristone (formerly called RU-486). This involves two pills being taken three days apart. The pills induce the woman's body to terminate the pregnancy and clear her uterus, this is done at home and a follow up visit a few days later is made to make sure that the abortion was completed.

While abortion is federally legal in the U.S., physicians who perform abortions are restricted by the regulations of their state's Medical Association. They typically do not permit abortions after twenty or twenty-one week gestation unless the woman's health or life is seriously at risk.[103]

In some states, you cannot get an abortion without Parental Consent (permission from a parent if you are a minor) or Parental Notification (having to tell a parent – but not get their permission – if you are a minor).

Calling a local, recognized and legitimate clinic will help answer any questions you have.

Abortions should be performed ONLY by qualified doctors.

When done safely by a responsible practitioner, abortion is perfectly safe – especially when done within the first thirteen weeks of pregnancy.

It is safe.

It is not easy.

Abortion is an emotional and physical taxing experience. It should not be considered a primary method of birth control. Abortion should be reserved only after other safer sex methods have been tried (or one of them has failed). Using abortion as the primary method of birth control should be considered irresponsible.

A SPECIAL NOTE ABOUT CONDOMS

- Condoms are the only contraceptives that help prevent both pregnancy and the spread of sexually transmitted diseases (including HIV) when used properly and consistently.

- Condoms are one of the most reliable methods of birth control when used properly and consistently.

- Condoms are widely available. You don't need a prescription or a doctor's visit, and they are not expensive.

- Condoms are discreet and convenient.

- Condoms have none of the medical side-effects some other birth control methods may have.

- Condoms are only needed when you are having sex, unlike some other contraceptives which require you to take or have them all of the time.

- If you have unprotected heterosexual sex, you have a 90% chance of getting pregnant – With proper condom use it drops almost to 2%.[104/105]

While having sex, remember to check occasionally that your condom is still on. Do this by reaching down and feeling for the condom's ring around the base of your penis.

If your condom comes off during sex or you find that it broke:

- Do not panic.

- Inform your partner immediately.

- Remove it if you can (or help them to).

- If your partner is a female, help her access emergency contraception within the first seventy-two hours.

- If you are the receptive partner, secure Post-Exposure Prophylaxis within the first seventy-two hours.

- Reevaluate your choice of condom size as well as your technique to ensure it was not due to user error.

- Get tested.

THE TEN COMMANDMENTS OF CONDOMS

THOU SHALT PUT THEM ON BEFORE THERE IS ANY SEXUAL CONTACT

This means USE THEM EVERY TIME.

Gay or straight.

Front or back.

Night or day.

Because sperm can be present in pre-cum.

And because pregnancy is not the only thing condoms protect against.

THOU SHALT MIND EXPIRATION DATES

They have them for a reason.

If it doesn't have one, do not use it.

THOU SHALT CHOOSE YOUR CONDOMS RESPONSIBLY

Only use condoms with reputable names.

Avoid "natural" or "lambskin" or anything with a scent (flavors and colors may be O.K.).

Do not be tempted by sizes – wearing a condom that is too big is almost as dangerous as not wearing one at all. Buy the condom that fits your penis, not your ego.

THOU SHALT BE NICE TO YOUR CONDOMS

Use only water based or silicone lubricant – nothing with oil of any kind in it.

Do not use more than one at a time/ no doubling up.

Store them in your bag/ nightstand/ bathroom – not in cars, wallets or pockets.

THOU SHALT AVOID CONDOMS WITH SPERMICIDE

Studies have found that they are not that much more effective for preventing pregnancy than non-spermicidal condoms, but may increase the risk of disease because of irritation that can come from some spermicide (specifically nonoxynol-9).

THOU SHALT KEEP THEM HANDY

The more available they are, the more likely they will be used.

THOU SHALT PUT THEM ON PROPERLY

Be sure to roll them the right way/ no flipping (see above re: pre-cum)

Pinch the tip to create a pocket.

(Guys with foreskin, pull it back before you put the condom on).

THOU SHALT REMOVE THEM PROPERLY

Hold at the base when removing.

Remove after you pull out/ before you go soft.

Tie off before throwing away – no flushing and not on the floor.

THOU SHALT BE GENEROUS WITH YOUR FRIENDS

Share! Because the more available they are, the more likely they will be used.

THOU SHALT PRACTICE, PRACTICE, PRACTICE…

Try alone…In the dark… one-handed, etc.… because you want to know you know what you're doing before you need to be doing it.

It is important, while practicing on your own, to pay attention to how long it takes your penis to detumesce (get soft) after you come…that is how long you will have to pull out when you are using them with someone else.

Buying condoms is good practice for being a responsible adult, plus you can experiment with different brands until you find a kind that you like.

SECTION VII – SEXUAL HEALTH

Chapter 32

RESPONSIBILITY
(THE SEVEN THINGS)

There are seven things that need to be met, in order for a sexual interaction to be considered responsible.

1) Privacy

2) Consent

Consent can be defined as an on-purpose, sober, chosen, informed, mutual, honest, and obvious agreement.

The rules of consent:

- It is the responsibility of the person initiating a sex act to obtain clear consent. Whenever you are unsure if consent has been given, ask.

- Consent cannot be manipulated. True consent means people are allowed to say "No".

- Consent is a process, which must be asked for every step of the way; if you want to move to the next level of sexual intimacy, that needs to be agreed on, too.

- Giving consent ahead of time does not waive a person's right to change their mind or say no later.

- Consent is never implied and cannot be assumed, even in the context of a relationship. Just because you are in a relationship does not mean that you have permission to have sex with your partner.

- A person who is intoxicated cannot legally give consent. If you're too drunk to make decisions and communicate with your partner, you're too drunk to consent.

- A person too far below your age range cannot legally give consent.

- A person in a lower position of authority cannot give consent to someone with a higher power differential.

- The absence of a "no" does not mean, "yes."

- Consent is not just about getting a yes or no answer, but about understanding what a partner is feeling.

- It is not sexy to have sex without consent!

3) Age Appropriateness

Specifically, the state or region in which you live most likely has more specific guidelines around age appropriateness and ages of consent. It is wise to be aware of these before you choose to engage in sexual activity.

For those still in high school, a good, general, guideline would be to:

- limit all sexual activities to people close to (read: within two years of) your own age.

- limit your sexual activities to non-penetrative acts until age sixteen.

- Reserve "varsity level" sex acts to people whom you know well, have ongoing caring feelings for, and who are willing and insistent on safer sex practices.

For those over the age of eighteen:

Once you are over the age of eighteen, **The Age Rule** kicks in and will be applicable for the rest of your life.

Take your age.

Divide it in half.

Add nine.

This will help to ensure that you engage in sexual/ romantic relationships with people within your general cohort. As we get older, age differences become less important. For example, a fourty-two year-old and a thirty-eight year-old's lives probably don't look that different. Likewise, a twenty-nine year-old and twenty-six year-old are probably going through the same general life stages. But a twenty-two year-old and a twenty year-old's lives should look and feel very different. Even a nineteen-year-old and an eighteen-year-old are potentially living very different lives especially if one has moved out of their parent's house or started college, or one is still in high school, but the other has graduated.

4) Foreplay

5) Safer Sex

6) Afterplay

7) The Big R (AKA: Relationship/Respect/Reciprocation)

Sexual morality is not about when you are allowed to have sex – it is about how you treat people when you are in sexual contact with them.

There is no realistic way to make a list of rules that will apply and be useful to ALL people in ALL situations, cultures, times or places. This is why it is important to act with respect – that Big R we talked about.

Another Big R is relationship. Many of you will most likely have sex with someone along the way that you are not "in love with." But as long as you have some kind of relationship with them, perhaps that is O.K. There may be hook-ups, "benefriend" situations or even sexual relationships that turn into romantic ones.

One-night stands happen. Hook-ups don't have to automatically equal "unhealthy." However, respect and reciprocity (fairness) still needs to happen if they are to be considered healthy. If one partner is having a one-night stand and the other thinks it is the beginning of something bigger, that is a problem.

The Big R looks different to different people in different situations, cultures, etc.

Morality is relative. That means what is O.K. for some people, in some places, at some times, is not O.K. for, in or at others.

- Do you cheat?

- Do you have sex with someone who is cheating on someone else?

- Do you tell someone if you have an STI?

- Do you go out with or have sex with someone when it clearly means something more to them than it does to you?

- Do you lie about your age or experience?

- Do you hook up with someone who is drunk?

These are important questions to ask ourselves.

There is no such thing as casual sex if you go at it from a respectful place – all sexual interactions that involve respect have meaning – whether it be a sweet moment with someone you'll never see again, a chance to learn something you wouldn't have otherwise, the start of something incredible that lasts the rest of your life, or just a fond memory to remember when you're older.

The bottom line is:

In order to go at sexual and intimate interactions from a respectful place:

- Act in a way that you would want to be treated.

- Err on the side of caution

and

- Do everything you can to not do something that could, would or might harm someone else (including yourself).

Chapter 33

PREVENTION

Because contraceptives are the best protection we have against most STIs and pregnancy it is, therefore, important to use them every time you have sex.

Prevention and safety should be shared between both people…

…Just like the babies and bugs would be.

Prevention means:

- Being open and honest with your partners, and being willing to have hard conversations. If you have (or suspect you may have) an STI of any kind-you must tell before your pants are removed.

- Getting tested (and insisting that your partners do as well).

- Not having sex under the influence of substances

- and using protection EVERY TIME.

A SPECIAL NOTE ABOUT TESTING

It is important

- To have a healthy, working relationship with our bodies.

- To not be afraid of them.

- To ask questions when something seems amiss.

Getting checkups for STI's and practicing safer sex is important. This is done by making an appointment with your doctor or local sexual health center, to discuss birth control, tests and treatment for sexually transmitted infections, and information about your sexual health.

This is especially important if you are worried you have been exposed to an STI or may have gotten someone pregnant.

Chapter 34

SELF-EXAMS

Testicular self-exam

Testicular cancer is the most common cancer for guys between the ages of fifteen to thirty-four.[106]

The test is done by looking at your scrotum. This is best done during a hot shower or bath, when the sac is most relaxed and pliable. Gently feel each testicle, rolling it between your fingers and checking for any lumps, bumps or changes in shape or size since your last examination.

Things to watch for are:

- Painless lumps

- Fluid in your scrotum

- Blood in your urine

- Changes in size

- Dull aches in your groin (for no obvious reason)

- Sharp pains should also be checked out by a doctor.

Testicular cancer is fairly easily cured, but, as with most cancers, early detection is important. Every guy over the age of fourteen should be doing this once per month.[107] This is especially important if you were born with an undescended testicle (which means that it didn't drop until you were six or you needed surgery).

Breast Self-Exam

Everyone should be doing this – even boys.

It becomes much more important if you are actually a female, if you are over the age of thirty-five and if breast cancer runs in your family.

But everyone should be doing this, because boys get breast cancer too.[108]

The best time to do this is in the shower. During a breast exam, feel for any lumps, bumps or changes in your breast tissue since the last time you checked (and, yes you have breast tissue). Feeling the breast is important as well as is looking at your breast in the mirror. There are many places online to find guidelines with which to do this, but basically you will be looking for:

- Painless lumps

- Changes in shape or size

- Differences in shape (between the left and right)

- Dimples or tucks that were not previously there

- Redness or scaliness, like dry skin

Doctors or online resources can be helpful if you have questions.

Early detection is important to save lives.

Chapter 35

A LIST OF SEX ACTS IN DEGREE OF RISK

- Fantasy

- Masturbation

- Hugging

- Holding hands

- Dry kissing

- Fondling

- Outercourse/ Dry sex

- Mutual Masturbation

- Wet kissing

- Mouth-penis contact with condom

- Mouth-vulva contact with barrier

- Mouth-anus contact with barrier

- Mouth-penis contact no condom/ no ejaculation

- Vaginal penetration with condom

- Hand-penis/ Hand-vulva contact

- Hand-anus contact

- Mouth-vulva contact no barrier

- Mouth-anus contact no barrier

- Mouth-penis contact no condom/ with ejaculation

- Anal penetration with condom

- Vaginal intercourse without condom

- Anal intercourse without condom

CONTRACT FOR A SAFE/ HEALTHY SEXUAL LIFE

Pregnancy and the infection of HIV and other sexually transmitted infections make sexual involvement a serious decision. Intercourse and other forms of sex could be hazardous to my health and the health of my partners.

If and when I choose to become sexually active, I agree to the following:

- I will never force or pressure anyone into sexual contact, and will always get clear consent from my partners.

- I will avoid making sexual decisions while under the influence of substances and will not allow myself to be pressured into doing anything sexual.

- I will have a relationship with my own body. I will keep it as healthy as possible, and work to figure out what is pleasurable to me before I share it with others. I will wash it, examine it, and have it tested.

- I will not use sex as an escape or a weapon, and understand that engaging in sexual activity does not prove that I am an adult, that I am straight or gay or that I am in love with anyone.

- I will discuss my sexual history with my partner/s. I will ask my partner's about their past sexual behavior. I will get vaccinated against the infections that I am able to and get a full STI screen once a year for the rest.

- I will always practice safer sex.

- I will encourage those I care about to do the same.

- I acknowledge that masturbation is the easiest/ safest way to avoid sexually transmitted infections and pregnancy. I understand that abstinence (though more difficult) can achieve the same result.

- I acknowledge that abstinence only works until it doesn't. I understand that I will be sexually active at some point, and can and may change my mind about my status as abstinent at any time. I will work to educate myself about sex and sexuality regardless of my current level of sexual activity.

When I choose to become sexually active, it will be done only after I have thought through the consequences of my actions, have gotten permission from (and discussed it with) my partner and have prepared to participate safely.

SECTION VIII – SEXUAL HARM

Chapter 36

HARASSMENT

A definition of what exactly sexual harassment is hard to pin down, and as flexible as there are people.

Sexual harassment can be defined as unwelcome attention of a sexual nature. It includes a range of behavior from mild transgressions and annoyances to serious abuses, which can (but definitely does not have to) include forced sexual activity.

There are two forms of sexual harassment we must all strive to avoid.

The first and most obvious form is **inappropriate sexual behavior.** Many times this is about failing to gain consent before touching others, or ignoring them when they have clearly not given consent. Inappropriate behavior can also be about our words rather than our actions. Talking to or toward someone in a sexual way, when they have not told or shown you that they are O.K. with that, can be harassment as well.

Notice I said, "talking toward someone," not "talking WITH someone." When conversation or attention is one-sided that is usually a signal that you are moving out of the category of appropriate.

Such acts could lead others to believe that if they comply, there will be benefits or if they do not comply with your wishes or endure your sexual comments or behaviors, there could be negative consequences.

The second form of sexual harassment concerns **making the general environments in which we live, work, learn and play uncomfortable for others.** This is easier to make mistakes about. Actions such as telling lewd jokes, taking or displaying sexually explicit photos, teasing a classmate or roommate or workmate about sexual matters, telling or posting sexual stories or comments can be perceived as offensive, degrading or intimidating. This could someone impact someone else's experience of our workplace, classroom, locker room, etc.

As for offenses that are not verbal, sexual assault means forced sexual contact, which can range from touching to kissing to penetration.

Chapter 37

ABUSE

Sexual abuse can be defined as:

A violation of trust in a relationship with

- Unequal power and/or advanced knowledge

- The need for secrecy

And

- Sexualized activity (sexualized not necessarily sexual)[109]

Whenever one person dominates and exploits another person through sexual activity or suggestion, using sexual feelings and behavior to degrade, humiliate, control, injure or misuse, this qualifies as sexual abuse.[110]

This can include violations of a position of trust, power and protection against those who lack a well-enough developed, emotional and intellectual "immune system," and promotes sexual secrecy among its victims.

Covert sexual abuse is more subtle and indirect.[111] Examples include inappropriate comments that shame or scare someone for or about the kind of person they are.

Overt sexual abuse involves direct touching, fondling and intercourse, against a person's will. Examples include kissing, fellatio, sodomy (anal penetration), penetration with objects, genitals or fingers, and masturbation. Use of force is typically involved – though this does not mean it always physical or violent.

A lot of abuse is about unfair power differentials such as age or physical power but could also involve emotional power, intellectual power or social power, along with numerous manipulative techniques.

Abuse involves secrecy, bribery, trickery, lies, threats and force.

Abusers AND victims can be:

- Male or female
- Adults or children or teens
- Someone known or a stranger

Sexual abuse can cause negative feelings such as confusion, fear, anger, shame, depression and worthlessness.

Sexual abuse can also cause positive feelings such as being special, paid attention to, noticed and loved, as well as physical pleasure.

Sexual abuse is not necessarily violent in all situations – exposure to pornography for example can be considered sexual abuse.

Sexual abuse can be:

Hands-on (kissing to touching to penetration, etc.)

Or

Hands-off (exposure to sexual body parts or acts, being watched or photographed in vulnerable situations, etc.)

An act may be defined as a sex crime depending on:

1) The level of consent

2) Age

3) Kinship

4) Sex

5) The nature of the act

6) The offender's intention

7) Geography

All of these factors have to do with society's views at any given time, which change and can be very different from place to place.

Cross-culturally, very few acts are universally offensive.

The prevalence of childhood sexual abuse is remarkably high for both boys and girls.

According to National Center for Missing and Exploited Children, 20% of all children are molested before the age of eighteen.[112]

Most abuse occurs prior to age sixteen.

Almost two thirds of that occurs before the age of twelve.

And more than half of that occurs before age six.[113]

30-40% of sexually abused children are asymptomatic following abuse.

30% exhibit few symptoms.

Leaving another approximate third that can be considered traumatized.[114]

EXAMPLES OF THE TRAUMATIC
EFFECTS OF ABUSE

- Anxiety/ Panic attacks

- Depression

- Distractibility/ Difficulty concentrating

- Guilt/shame

- Insomnia

- Intimacy issues/lost of trust

- Irritability/ anger

- Loss of self esteem

- Memory loss

- Negative body image/ eating disorders

- Nightmares/ flashbacks

- Numbing/ apathy

- Poor choice in future partners/ victim stance

- Promiscuity

- Self-mutilation/harm

- Sexual dysfunction

- Shock/ denial

- Social withdrawal/ isolation

- Substance abuse

- Suicidal ideation/ attempts

Traumatized victims of abuse can act two ways:

1) Socially afraid and cut off from intimacy.

Self-esteem issues and sexual dysfunction can also be results of abuse, like guilt about arousal or appearance, inability to talk about sex, shame in general and physical difficulties with excitement or orgasm.

Or

2) Over-compensating with numerous partners.

Promiscuity (having sex with lots of different people) can come to mean power for survivors of abuse, as can abusive activity – both giving and receiving.

Things like sexual pleasure can become confusing, because sometimes, sexual abuse can feel pleasurable when it is happening.

When this happens, the lines between appropriate and inappropriate may become blurry and mess with dating skills and behaviors, like knowing when-to-kiss or when-not-to-kiss, or how to tell when touch should end in sex and when it doesn't need to end in sex (or even should not end in sex).

Many guys do not even believe that boys can be offended against sexually. And when they are offended by a female, it can be especially confusing becomes it is sometimes not even seen as abuse.

Can you say LeTourneau?

Other things, which make male sexual abuse especially traumatic, are that:

- Male victims are more likely to grow up and act their abuse out on others.

- This is in large part because boys who are abused are less likely to talk about it than girls, and, therefore, less likely to seek counseling or be given help.[115]

Any child, who is abused and/or made to do sexual things with an adult is not to blame – even if they consented to the abuse at the time, cared about their abuser or even enjoyed parts of it.

Sex acts during sex offenses is NOT what sex is.

Chapter 38

ASSAULT

Sexual assault takes many forms including attacks such as rape as well as any unwanted sexual contact or threats.

Usually a sexual assault occurs when someone touches any part of another person's body in a sexual way (even through clothes) without that person's consent or permission.

Some types of sexual acts, which fall under the category of sexual assault, include forced sexual intercourse (rape), sodomy (oral or anal sexual acts), molestation (touching), incest, and fondling.

Sexual assault in any form can be a devastating crime. Assailants can be strangers, acquaintances, friends, or family members. They commit sexual assault by way of violence, threats, coercion, manipulation, pressure or tricks.

Basically, almost any sexual behavior a person has not consented to, and that causes that person to feel uncomfortable, frightened or scared can be included in the sexual assault category.

The law generally assumes that a person does not consent to sexual contact if he/ she is:

- Forced

- Threatened

- Tricked

- Unconscious

- Drugged

- Under certain, specific ages

- Developmentally delayed

- Chronically, mentally ill

Examples of this can include

- Someone putting their finger, tongue, mouth, penis or an object in your body that you do not want them to.

- Someone touching, fondling, kissing or making any unwanted contact with your body that you do not want them to.

- Someone forcing you to perform oral sex or forcing you to receive oral sex.

- Someone forcing you to look at sexually explicit material (including a random picture of a penis texted to your phone) or forcing or tricking you to pose for sexually explicit pictures

- A doctor, nurse, or other health care professional giving you an unnecessary examination or touching your body in an unprofessional, unwarranted and inappropriate manner.

Since every person and situation is different, victims of sexual assault will respond to an assault in different ways.

Many factors can influence an individual's response to, and recovery from, sexual assault. These may include

- The age and developmental maturity of the person who was victimized.

- The social support network available to the person who was victimized.

- The offender's relationship to the person who was victimized.

- The response to the attack by police, medical personnel, and parents.

- The frequency (how often it happened), severity (the level of violence and injury) and duration (how long it went on) of the assaults.

- The response by the criminal justice system.[116]

Some survivors of sexual assault will find ways to recover relatively quickly, while others will feel the lasting effects of their victimization throughout their lifetime.

Sexual assault is a frightening and traumatic situation.

However it is important to understand that someone who is victimized is not a victim.

When someone is assaulted it is not their fault.

A SPECIAL NOTE ABOUT GUYS AND RAPE

It is not just girls or guys in prison who are raped.

If you have experienced any unwanted sexual contact:

- Say something to someone who will listen – a parent, teacher, counselor or friend.

- Then call the police.

- Get medical attention to check for venereal disease, internal injuries, or (if you are female) the possibility of pregnancy.

- Do nothing that will change your appearance or the appearance of the place of the rape.

- Do not take a bath or shower.

- Don't even wash your hands.

- Take a change of clothes with you to the hospital.

- Report the crime to the police as soon as possible

- Write as much as you can remember about your attack and the circumstances.

The necessary evidence must be collected immediately.

The decision to press any charges does not.

Being raped or molested does not make you weak (even if you felt powerless). Though many guys who have been raped have difficulty discussing it, it is just as important to talk to someone as it is for everyone else. Talking to someone can lessen our own trauma as well as to prevent them from harming anyone else.

Being raped or molested does not make you gay (even if there were parts that may have been enjoyable). Genitals feel good when they are touched. It is as simple as that. Some guys can become aroused and even come during manipulated or forced sex acts.

Choices can be taken from anyone, but if we surround ourselves with supportive people – both personal and professional – it can help.

ANOTHER NOTE ABOUT GUYS AND RAPE

Again, anyone can be victimized. It is our responsibility to protect ourselves – this is particularly important for females, because they are the victims of sexual crime a majority of the time.

However, this does not mean that it is women's responsibility to prevent rape.

This is primarily the guys' job.

Because, though most men will never rape in their lifetimes – most offenders are males.[117]

Why is this important for you to understand?

Because very few people who victimize others planned to grow up and do that.

What can we, as men do?

- Choose to not be that guy.

- Accept that "no" means no. And accept that a lot of other things. That "maybe" means no, that "wait" means no – that nothing other than "yes" means "yes," until we are shown very clearly otherwise.

- Make choices about the ways you consider the roles of males as well as females and ideas about masculinity and femininity.

- Do not hang with sexually aggressive, criminal or violent peers.

- Do not put up with words like "slut" and "whore," these words are essentially unfair because there is no male equivalent. It is unfair for a girl to be called a slut if she chooses to do sexual things with five guys, if a guy who did the same thing would get a high-five.

- Pay attention to your drug and alcohol usage. Substances make us do lots of things we would not do sober.

- Pay attention to your level of impulsivity and ability to delay gratification in general. If you have any sort of attention-deficit issues, handle it responsibly.

- Pay attention to the porn you watch, and its portrayal of both women and men.

- If you have been abused, molested or raped – deal with it – talk to someone.

- Do not allow your friends to be that guy.

- Do not promote rape jokes, rape games, rape music or other aspects of "rape culture." Monitor your family and cultural values, judgments and feelings about women-particularly if they revolve around women being targets of hostility, violence or viewed as less-than, as property or as only-there-for-sex. Ideas around males being dominant and it being the girl's job to get guys off also contribute to rape culture mentality.

- Be a good friend – everyone knows someone who has been sexually abused. If your friends are not sharing these types of things with you, that may be a sign that you are not viewed as someone sensitive to these issues. This is worth investigating.

- On that note, support those you know who have been abused, both female and male.

- Do not engage in anyone's oppression, based on race, national origin, language, age, level of disability, sex, gender or orientation.

Chapter 39

PERSONAL SAFETY

PROACTIVE TIPS

Things you can do ahead of time to keep yourself safe and lessen the chances of being victimized.

- Be aware that walking alone at night may be dangerous.

- Observe constantly – do not engage in behaviors that restrict your observation. (Good men do not walk up quietly behind someone when it is obvious they are unaware).

- Walk with your head up and a confident stride.

- Stay in well-lit areas.

- Trust your gut. If something feels weird, it probably is.

- Have a plan: someone to call for a ride, extra cash for a cab

- Always dress so that movement is not restricted.

- Know your routes: Notice lighting, alleys, abandoned buildings, and street people.

- Try to vary your routine routes of travel. Don't let your behavior be too predictable.

- If you are alone and worry you are being followed or you see a person or group further down the street that makes you feel uncomfortable, cross the street, walk in another direction, or ask other people walking if you may walk or stay with them for a while.

- When walking to your door or apartment, carry your keys in your hand. Don't stand in the doorway and fumble with your keys. Have them ready to use.

- While waiting for public transportation, keep your back against a wall (or pole) so that you cannot be surprised from behind.

- Elevators are safer than stairs, though trust your gut if you are alone and isolated and there is someone else on the lift. (Good men do not feel offended when a female crosses the street or chooses a different elevator).

- When parking your car, note your position carefully, so that you can go directly to it.

- When returning to your car, look around. If you notice anything or anyone suspicious, go back the way you came.

- If you have electric locks know how to unlock the driver's door only (as opposed to all the doors at the same time).

- If you return to your car and find it parked next to a big van – especially one without side windows, enter your car from the passenger door or wait and come back later.

- Do not park next to big vans – especially those with no side windows.

- As soon as you get into your car, lock the doors and leave.

- Make a habit of not letting your gas indicator fall below the quarter-full mark.

- If you run out of gas or have an accident, don't take rides from strangers. If a stranger wants to help, ask them to call a repair truck or police for you (if you haven't already).

- If you see an accident or stranded motorist and you are alone, it is probably more helpful to call 911 on your cell phone rather than stop.

- Hitchhiking is NEVER safe.

- Neither is picking up hitchhikers – Do not allow strangers into your car.

- Do not allow strangers into your home.

- Avoid letting strangers know that you are home alone.

- And never go outside to investigate a strange noise (we've all seen that movie).

- Always let someone know where you are going and what you are doing and when you will be back – especially trips, parties, first dates, etc… this is especially important when meeting an online acquaintance for the first time.

- While getting to know someone, keep dates to public places like restaurants, malls, theaters, etc.

- Group dates are great when you first start getting to know someone.

- Travel in groups as often as possible – especially when going to parties or clubs.

- Contract with friends to stay together.

- Don't break your contracts.

- Realize how much drinking increases your risk of something bad happening. Understand your limitations around substances.

- Do not leave food or drink unattended in public places-especially parties/ bars.

A SPECIAL NOTE ABOUT DATE RAPE DRUGS

Date rape drugs are chemicals usually put into someone's drink, which weaken you, impair your ability to move or remember things.

There are three main kinds

- Gamma Hydroxybutyrate (GHB)

- Rohypnol also called Rophys (pronounced "Roofies")

- Ketamine Hydrochloride[118]

They are typically colorless and odorless and can be easily slipped into drinks such as soda or alcohol without being detected.

- Do not accept drinks that are handed to you by someone you don't know well (unless you saw it being made).

- Don't leave your drink unattended, if you must leave it-leave it with a trusted friend to guard or get a new one when you come back.

- Be aware of your surroundings and trust our gut.

If you taste or see anything strange in your drink or begin to feel strange:

- Stop drinking immediately.

- Let someone nearby know what you suspect happened (these chemicals can begin working very quickly).

- Ask them to call the police.

At some point, someone may offer you one of these for recreational use or because "it makes sex better."

Do not do that under any circumstances.

REACTIVE TIPS

Things you can do when/ if something bad happens.

- Accept that at some point in your life, someone will try to seriously harm you in some way.

- Remember that most people who are victimized know their rapists.[119]

- Remember that, if you have poor instincts or boundaries, you can be easily manipulated.

- If you are mugged, throw wallets or bag away from you (the attacker is probably more interested in the money than you). Carrying a fake wallet is a great idea.

- When you can, run.

- When you run, run loud.

- If you are attacked, and there is no safe alternative (like running), then decide to defend yourself and do it immediately.

- Take the fight to them – cut off their attack and incapacitate them. Do this loudly.

- The elbow is the strongest point in your body, if you are close enough to use it-use it.

- Failing elbows – thumbs.

- Go for the squishy parts – eyes and balls. Try to take out their vision and/or wind.

- Strike with total disregard for their safety.

- And never regret anything you do to save your own life.

- Self-defense classes are a really good idea for everyone.

SECTION IX – ONLINE SAFETY

Chapter 40

EXPOSURE

In the global village that is the World Wide Web, a plethora of information is available at our fingertips. This includes information, art and entertainment. Unfortunately this also includes sometimes – false information, a good deal of pornography, racist, sexist, homophobic and other bigoted or violent information and images.

ANOTHER NOTE ABOUT PORNOGRAPHY

Porn, in particular, has a much different meaning than it did just a generation ago.

- Pornography used to be relatively hard to come by.

In the late seventies, the average age of first exposure to pornography was sixteen. The average age of pornography exposure today is estimated at eleven.[120] According to a 2007 study from the University of Alberta, as many as 90% of boys and 70% of girls have been exposed to sexually explicit content at least once by the time they enter puberty[121]. This often happens accidentally – such a while completing their homework.

Not only has porn moved from being an adult commodity, but its frequency and intensity have both had their volumes turned up as it has seeped into most every area of popular American culture.

- Pornography used to be relatively tame/ vanilla.

There are very few kids who will not encounter pornography at some point by the time they begin high school, some puberty[122], most certainly by the time they graduate. Magazines that are legally restricted for adults are still kept behind those little plastic dividers in convenience stores and require ID for purchase, but obscene materials that could be illegal even for adults are easily accessed online.

Young people today actually have to expend more energy to avoid pornography these days than their dads ever spent trying to get their hands on the stuff back in the day.

Several factors contribute to this:

- The financial rewards for the producers who can make money from people's insecurities and natural inquisitiveness.

- The lack of a walled village online for young people.

- The technology available to underagers and your knowledge of how to navigate them (iPorn/ PSP/ telephones).

- The ease of posting and downloading amateur or homemade images and text as well as the pay-to-see stuff.

- Unsolicited push-porn such as pop-up ads, banners and keyword searches make even innocent and legitimate pages and searches pathways to pornography exposure.

It is difficult to say how this hypersexuality is going to affect young people who:

- Have not yet developed the ability (or even the motivation) to navigate relationships

- May not have had any other education around sex or safety

- Are still impressionable and have yet to solidify their self-concepts

- Have bodies (as well as their brains) that have not yet fully developed.

Porn is something to consider carefully because of:

- the addictive nature of porn for many people

- the expense

- as well as privacy risks

- and the ways in which porn can morph gender ideas in negative ways and interfere with (or even prevent) the forming of healthy, relationships

Avoiding exposure is most likely not realistic.

- Every second, $3,075.64 is being spent on pornography.

- At any given moment almost 30,000 people in this country are viewing pornography

- A new pornographic video is created once an hour[123]

- Lube has twice as many Google hits as toothpaste.

- Orgy has twice as many hits as condoms.

It is important, however, to make sure that you work to not let it misshape your values or your self-esteem.

Be aware of how porn can impact our expectations around sex, sexuality and relationship.

Do not let it taint the ways you view yourselves and treat each other.

Chapter 41

EXPLOITATION

According to the Crimes Against Children Research Center, one out of five U.S. teenagers who are active online, have received an unwanted sexual solicitation via the Web. Solicitations were defined as

- requests to engage in sexual activities

- sexual talk

- requests to give personal sexual information.

Only 25% of those told a parent.

One third of American teens have received an aggressive sexual solicitation in the past year. This means a predator

- asked a young person to meet somewhere

- called a young person on the phone, and/or

- sent them correspondence, money, or gifts through the U.S. Postal Service.

77% of the targets for online predators are fourteen years of age or older.

22% are aged ten to thirteen.[124]

The U.S. Department of Justice maintains that, on average, there is one child molester per square mile in the United States.[125] Given isolated areas such as Kansas or the Appalachians and the vastness of places such as Texas or Alaska, this may not seem like such a big deal, however if you acknowledge that the Web transforms your computer screen into an open window between your home and virtually anyplace else in the world with electricity, these stats take on new meanings.

Report sexual exploitation, harassment, abuse and threats

- To your Internet service provider

- To the CyberTipline online or 1-800-843-5678.

- To your local police

- To your parents

Chapter 42

THE WEB

Some web sites are cool, others are lame, and some contain so-called "adult" content, others are demeaning, racist, sexist, hateful and violent or contain false information. These sites contain material that can be disturbing, even for adults.

- When this happens, it's best to immediately leave by clicking on the Home icon, going to another site, or shutting down your browser.

Web sites sometimes ask for information about yourself. Don't ever tell anyone online your full name, your parents' names, your home address, your school name or location, your phone number, social security or credit card number. If someone asks you for this info don't give it to them and report the incident.

- Never give out any information about yourself or your family without first checking with your parents.

- Never give out any information about your friends without their consent.

- This includes pictures.

Some web sites ask your permission to download a program or "plug-in." In some cases these programs can be used to display unwanted advertising on your computer but they can also invade your privacy by tracking what you're doing online, planting viruses and increasing your risk of being hacked.

- Don't download anything unless you're certain it is from a trustworthy source.

Chapter 43

CHAT

Chat is possibly the most dangerous area on the Internet.[126] People are not always who they seem to be. The basic rules for online safety apply to all areas of the Internet, but they are especially important in chat areas.

- As with other areas of the Internet, you don't know who is there, so never say anything in a chatroom that you wouldn't say in public.

- Again, never give personal information to anyone you don't know.

- Remember, chat (like email and texts) can easily be copied and forwarded to others. If you do send personal information to friends, be sure that they are willing to respect your privacy.

- Chatrooms are typically organized around topics, so avoid any topic area that makes you feel uncomfortable.

- Avoid people that try to change the topic from the one for which it is designed – particularly is the topics are sexual, illegal or make you feel uncomfortable.

Chapter 44

SOCIAL NETWORKING

Some people have their own web sites or sites maintained by their school or an organization. If you do post something on the web, be sure to never include your home address, telephone number. Be careful regarding posting photographs. If you do want people to be able to contact you through the web, email is safer.

Some services encourage you to post a profile with information such as your age, sex, hobbies, and interests. While such profiles can help you meet likeminded people, they can also make you the subject of harassment or worse, even if you don't post your name and address or other information that could lead to a physical contact.

- To be safe and avoid hassles it's better to keep your profiles set to private.

Some instant messaging software can also be used for video chat where you send your picture – in real time – along with your words.

- Be especially careful about using video or digital cameras when networking. Background images and scenery can provide predators clues to your identity and location.

- You don't have to respond to any messages that are rude, annoying, or make you feel uncomfortable.

Be sure you know with whom you are networking, and be aware that anything you type could be forwarded to other people. The Internet is forever.

A SPECIAL NOTE ABOUT SEXTING

Sending graphic images and pornographic videos via text message to friends. It's becoming such a problem that major cities have entire teams on their police forces dedicated to sexting and Internet crimes. This trend of sending sexual texts and pictures via cellular phone has led to a number of teens being charged with child pornography.

Under federal law, child pornography is a criminal act, and is defined as a visual depiction of any kind, including a drawing, cartoon, sculpture, painting, photograph, film, video, or computer-generated image or picture, which depicts a minor engaging in sexually explicit conduct and is obscene.[127] **These illegal images can be produced and presented in various forms including print media, videotape, film, CD, the Internet, and yes, cellular phones.**

No matter the circumstance, it is illegal to possess, distribute or manufacture pornography involving anyone less than eighteen years of age. Therefore, teens found distributing or possessing such images can be found guilty of child pornography.

It is also important to remember that, although sexting is generally done between friends – it does not always stay that way. Once something is sent over Internet or telephone lines, you lose all control over what happens to it. Any picture, text, email or web page you create, send, pass on or have any connection to could exist (and be traced back to you) in perpetuity (that means forever).

The Internet is forever.

CONTRACT FOR RESPONSIBLE INTERNET USE

I understand that the Internet is a tool, and (though it can be entertaining) should not be viewed as a toy. As with weapons or automobiles, serious harm can result from using it in irresponsible ways.

I understand that the Internet is forever.

- I will not create sexual, violent or offensive screen names, avatars or profiles.

- I will not post or send pictures of myself (or others) in compromising, illegal, unethical, inappropriate or otherwise questionable positions.

- I will never post or send pictures of myself in the nude.

- I will not post any pictures of others without their permission.

- I will not share my password with anyone.

I understand that anonymity gives financial, emotional, physical and sexual predators more access to prey.

- I will not give out personal information to anyone online, including my full name, address, passwords, phone number, social security or credit card numbers (or anyone else's).

- I will beware of others trying to start conversations in chat rooms about something other than the topic for which the chat room was designed. I will be cautious when someone attempts to turn a conversation sexual. I will avoid others who refuse to hear "no" or who ignore attempts to change the subject when I am uncomfortable.

- I will not make telephone contact with anyone I have met online, without the permission of my parents.

- I will not make physical contact with anyone I have met online without the permission of my parents and/ or someone to accompany me.

- I will never meet anyone I have met online in a non-public place, without telling someone I trust or without VERIFIED identification including name, phone number and school or place of work.

- I will not download anything unless I am certain that it is from a reliable source.

I understand that anonymity does not give me license to be cruel, rude or crude.

- I will be polite in my interactions online, using the same manners, language and level of respect that I would in public. I will not say anything in a chatroom, email, forum or post that I would not say in public.

- I will not reciprocate when others behave negatively and will remove myself from the situation if I become too angry.

- I will not stay silent when myself or someone else is harassed online. I will report violent, sexual and hate behaviors to administrators, parents and/or police when necessary.

I understand that one cannot "unsee" things.

- I will choose my websites and media carefully.

- I will generally avoid things that make me uncomfortable, and know that I can pause, stop and delete anything I wish, even if I have already begun downloading and /or viewing it.

- I will specifically avoid areas of the Web that focus on negative, inappropriate or unsafe sexual depictions, sites that promote hate speech, bigotry and other forms of prejudice, and sites whose main purposes revolve around violence and offensive behavior – especially when it promotes hatred or the oppression of or violence towards others based on race, national origin, language, age, level of disability, sex, gender or orientation.

I understand that pornography is inherently addictive, designed to be so, and that it generally depicts negative images of both males and females.

- I understand that pornography is unrealistic and that real people in real sexual situations do not look like, speak like, or act like the people in these films.

- I will not use pornography as sex education.

I understand that electronic communication is good for connecting with others, though not for active connection, good for passing information or time but not truly communicating.

- I will balance my online life with real-time, warm, human contact, socially responsible and age appropriate activities, relationships and physical exercise.

- I will keep my profile set to private.

- I will limit my social networking conversations to passing information and sharing news, not personal conversations or arguments.

I understand that not everything that is free is actually free.

- I will work to learn the consequences of both providing and downloading pirated and copyrighted materials.

- I realize that the motives for people who rip and share are not always altruistic.

- I will avoid participating in such behaviors and encourage others to do the same.

- I will chose to not steal from or diminish the work of artists – particularly those whom I admire.

I will follow these rules while online, regardless of how or where I am accessing the Internet.

When I choose to connect to or interact through the Internet, I will think through the consequences of my actions, understand the impact of my behavior on myself (as well as others), and behave appropriately, responsibly and safely – to protect my family, my friends and myself.

SECTION X – FOR PARENTS

Introduction

My name is Jo Langford.

I am a parent, therapist and sex educator in Seattle.

For the last twenty years I have worked to use information, education and humor to help underagers increase their knowledge and self-confidence as a proactive defense against the unfortunate consequences that sometimes accompany sexual activity.

We have an awful, awful reality right now.

Despite our resources, relatively decent standard of living and positive indices for life expectancy and education, America is one of the most unhealthy developed countries in this world with regard to sex and sexuality.

If you are the parent of an American teen:

- Somewhere around 300,000 of you may become grandparents before your child graduates high school.[128]

- Approximately half of your kids are already sexually active in some way.[129]

- A quarter of those children have gotten an STI[130]

- 33% of your children received an aggressive online solicitation from an online predator in the last year.[131]

- One out of every five of your sons has sent a picture of his penis to someone over telephone lines.[132]

As parents, we all spend a great deal of time being worried about sexual predators-it's on the front page of every paper, websites and news channels are loaded with messages and warnings, but most of the sexual damage being done to our young people is being done to each other and themselves.

The good news is this is preventable.

I would be shocked if anyone reading this was not supportive of defensive driving courses. The American National Standard Safe Practices for Motor Vehicle Operation defines Defensive Driving as "Driving to save lives, time and money, in spite of the conditions around you and the actions of others."[133]

Teenagers having sex doesn't scare me – they've done that since the beginning of time.

Actually, That is not completely true – teenagers having sex scares me in the same way teenagers driving scares me.

But I am a lot less worried when I am confident that a particular kid has

- learned how to drive properly

- and drive safely

- and that they have done everything they can to not have their driving impact their life (or the lives of the people they interact with) in a negative or adversely, life-changing way.

Traditional abstinence messages are not working –

- We would not teach our children how to drive by only explaining what we DON'T want them to do behind the wheel.

- We would not wait to tell them about seatbelts only when/if THEY inquired about them.

- We would not teach them how to drive, based on how we wish or hope OTHER people would behave on the freeways.

My goal is for this book to serve as a Defensive Sexuality course – Loving and relating, "to save lives, time and money, in spite of the conditions around you and the actions of others."

Educational interventions such as this, are needed that will provide skills and information which underagers need to protect themselves from unintended pregnancy and sexually transmitted infection when they do become sexually active – regardless of their age, identity or marital status.

This is time for real, tangible change in our children's level of sexual knowledge, education, and empowerment.

Let this book be an opportunity and catalyst to provide information so that your kids can make informed decisions and have the necessary tools to approach sex and sexuality with a sense of confidence and seriousness, having fun along the way, while doing as little harm to themselves and their peers as possible.

Chapter 45

THE STATISTICAL REALITY

The focus on abstinence-only education is primarily on encouraging kids to say no, but that is not consistent with adolescent biology, and teens are not saying no anymore than they ever have.

Research from four cycles of the National Survey of Family Growth, which studies information on sexual and marital behaviors, reports that almost all Americans have sex before marrying. According to non-marital sex research, this behavior is the norm in the U.S., and has been for the past fifty years.[134] A recent study published in Public Health Reports, shows that by age twenty, 75% of Americans have had non-marital sex.[135]

Teens do not refrain from sex just because they are scared or don't know how to protect themselves or have been given unhelpful or negative or shaming information.

The problem is not teens having sex.

The problem is

- Teens having unprotected sex

- Teens having unsafe sex

- Teens getting pregnant

- Teens getting sexually transmitted infections.

After the 1.5 billion dollars that has been spent thus far on abstinence-only education[136], we have learned that, **at best, abstinence-only education delays the onset of sexual activity by approximately six months.**[137]

We have also learned that, **when those same kids DO start to engage in non-marital sex** (as 95% of Americans do),

- They are less likely to use protection

- More likely to get pregnant than teens who have had more comprehensive sex ed.

- Abstinence-only students are also more likely to engage in anal and oral sex "to preserve their virginities."

The result? Our country has the highest rate of teenage pregnancy among the developed countries in the world.

- 750,000 teen girls are expected to become pregnant in the next year.

- 350,000 of these are between the ages of fifteen to seventeen.

- Half of these occur within six months of becoming sexually active.

- Over 80% of teen pregnancies are unintended[138].

Abstinence programs typically teach very little about condoms – other than failure rates, and even that is exaggerated, with some programs citing a "50%" failure rate for condoms.[139]

The message they are trying to send is abstinence, but the message received is often, "Why bother?"

Abstinence messages are not working –

- We would not teach our children how to drive by only explaining what we DON'T want them to do behind the wheel

- We would not tell them about seatbelts only if THEY inquired about them.

- We would not teach them how to drive, based on how we wish or hope OTHER people would behave on the freeways.

Three to four girls out of ten become pregnant in this country before they reach the age of twenty.

In Europe, where they

- Start having sex at the same time

- At the same rate,

- But talk about it in school,

- Post condom ads on billboards,

- And provide medically accurate information in magazines for kids and teens…

…The pregnancy rate is closer to six out of 100.[140]

The most common reasons American teens do not use contraception are:

- Not planning for sex

- Not believing pregnancy will occur

- Not wanting to use birth control

- Not knowing where to get birth control/ protection

- Not knowing how to practice safer sex

- Not feeling comfortable asking questions about sex in general

Each of these things is easily addressed with clear and open, factual and accurate, reality-based comprehensive sexual education.

Combating the rate of teen sex does not make sense – **the focus should be on avoiding negative consequences.**

With regard to sexuality many adolescents:

- Have never discussed sex or sexuality with a supportive adult with whom they can ask questions.

- Have more sex than they have knowledge.

- Do not understand the difference between sex that is healthy and safer and sex that is not.

- Have sex experiences long before they are mentally, emotionally and physically ready.

- Engage in sexual behavior to satisfy non-sexual needs (like control of a relationship, acceptance by others, increasing their self-esteem).

We need to provide skills and information our children need to protect themselves from unintended pregnancy and sexually transmitted infection when they do become sexually active – regardless of their age or marital status.

Acceptance of these realities, and giving them tools to help navigate this period, is a much more acceptable policy than giving kids information that is misleading or inaccurate, or based only on how we hope they behave.

These kids trust us.

As they should.

As we want them to.

Teens should be given opportunities to use their judgment, to exercise their critical thinking muscles, and to make their mistakes.

Because mistakes will be made – they are teenagers

BUT

- We can lessen their impacts.
- We can be there to support them.
- We can help them figure out what went wrong and how to fix it next time.

How does a responsible parent teach their kid to drive?

Simply tell them not to speed?

Explain how many times seatbelts don't work?

Abstinence is a good idea and should be encouraged, but it conflicts with the statistical reality we are dealing with, and relying on that as they only expectation is not serving our young people in this country.

Chapter 46

THE "GAY" ISSUE

Despite the nearly one million gay teenagers in the United States[141], and the growing acknowledgement of gays and lesbians in American popular culture, **gay and lesbian teens are particularly uninformed and alienated by sex education classes.**

Most school districts in this country advocate some form of sex education, but very few include resources and education for lesbians and gays in their curriculum. **In fact, often the only sex that is discussed (and which kids are encouraged to abstain from) is penis-in-vagina.**

A large problem with this, is a 2008 study out of the Bradley Hasbro Children's Research Center, which found that **more than half of fifteen to nineteen year olds have oral sex and that anal sex is increasing among straight teenagers and young adults** (in fact between 1995 and 2004, the number doubled). [142/143]

Straight kids participate in oral and anal sex:

- To avoid pregnancy

- To please a partner

- To preserve their virginity (which is referred to as "saddlebacking")

According to the Centers for Disease Control, the probability of HIV acquisition by the receptive partner in unprotected oral sex with an HIV carrier is one per 10,000 acts. In vaginal sex, it's 10 per 10,000 acts. In anal sex, it's 50 per 10,000 acts.[144]

This means, anal sex is five times more dangerous than vaginal sex and fifty times more dangerous than oral sex.

Abstinence education emphasizes the importance of virginity and only focuses on vaginal intercourse. Studies around sexual and reproductive health issues find that about 10% of the American teens have engaged in anal sex.[145]

Without the opportunity to be educated about the subject, some (especially straight) **teens conclude that oral and anal sex are not sex, and therefore must not have the same risks or consequences.** In fact it is often referred to without the word sex as in "Getting oral" or "We did anal last night." These practices are also called "saddlebacking" when used to mistakenly "preserve" virginity.

Worse still, some teens can convince themselves that anal sex between partners of the opposite sex does not carry the same risk as "gay sex", since it isn't "gay".

This mentality is a significant risk factor for HIV and other sexually transmitted infections. It's critical that we recognize that more and more young people are engaging in anal sex so we can open the lines of communications and help them protect their sexual health

Additionally, many states still embrace "abstinence-until-marriage" curricula, which specifies, "A mutually faithful monogamous relationship in the context of marriage is the expected standard of human sexuality."[146] The hope is that this will change over time, though, given that most gays and lesbian in this country are legally barred from the joys of marriage, an "abstinence until marriage," stance is insulting to promote to a percentage of the American populace that is roughly the same size as America's Jewish population.

According to the Sexuality Information and Education Council of the United States, thirty-three states require HIV and sexually transmitted infection education. Nine require that "discussion of sexual orientation be inclusive." Three states require "only negative information" about homosexuality (or "homosexual" acts).[147]

Not-straight kids have to navigate adolescence and puberty in isolation to avoid the stigma of negative stereotypes and biases inundated through and by mainstream popular culture.

Addressing gay issues and homosexuality in sex education could help:

- Minimize the harassment of gay and lesbian students as well as emotional isolation, which contributes to high suicide and dropout rates among gay teens. (40% of gay teens – as opposed to 10% of straight teens – have attempted suicide at least once, according to the American Journal of Public Health)[148]. They are four times as likely to succeed.[149]

- Address the heightened health risks faced by gays and lesbians (and those kids who do "gay and lesbian things") due to misinformation and lack of information about safer-sex practices

In addition to suicide behaviors, these kids are at increased risk for:

- Mental health issues

- Violence at home and school

- Harassment

- Substance abuse as escapism

- Pregnancy and disease. Gay kids are less likely than their straight counterparts to prepare for sexual encounters. Gay kids are more likely than straight kids to use sexual encounters as ways to either figure out if they are gay (or prove to others that they are not).

Counseling and sex education should address the full range of behaviors that teens engage in – whether gay or straight.

Chapter 47

ABSTINENCE-ONLY VS. COMPREHENSIVE SEX EDUCATION

Information from studies consistently report abstinence-only approaches do not work. Sex education trends tend to focus only on the risks and dangers, such as pregnancy, HIV, assault, and STI's. These reinforce negative feelings about sex, which act as barriers to reducing risk behaviors.

In April 2007, The U.S. government evaluated its own programs through a study by Mathematica Policy Research Inc.[150], and found:

- Approximately half of all high school youth reported having engaged in sexual activity.

- A quarter of those kids have a Sexually Transmitted Infection (STI).

Abstinence only education was found to have had

- No overall impact on teen sexual activity.

- No difference in the rate of unprotected sex.

Students in abstinence-only programs had similar age of sexual debut (14.9 months) as their control group peers.

The largest difference recorded between an abstinence-only program and the control group (which had no education) was a program called Recapturing the Vision. They reported 48% of teens in their program had remained abstinent in the previous twelve months.

The control group reported 43%.

The study found that there was some improved knowledge of STI's, however, it also discovered that the youth that participated in abstinence-only education programs were less likely to believe that birth control worked and so were less likely to use them.

University of Washington researchers found students who had comprehensive sex education were

- 60% less likely to become pregnant than those without any sex education

and

- 50% less likely than the abstinence-only group.[151]

Comprehensive sex education means:

Answering the questions honestly, medically accurate and age appropriate, while being consistent and respectful of the participants.

And includes information which addresses:

- Human development – age-appropriate information that addresses developmental stages.

- Personal skills – such as relationships, self-esteem and discussions around choice-making (which means choices need to be offered – not one option, abstinence only).

- Cultural-relevance – responding to and discussing what sexual behavior is actually happening.

- Diversity – keeping the language open, and focusing on the behaviors a person does, not judgments about who a person is.

- Sexual health – including safety practices, options and testing

- Reliable resources.

Comprehensive sex education

- Delays the onset of intercourse

- Improves the frequency and success of the use of safer sex practices.

- Does not lead to increased sexual activity[152]

Chapter 48

THE CALL

Knowledge and self-confidence are the best protection against the unfortunate consequences that sometimes accompany sexual activity.

More knowledge is better than not enough knowledge.

Therapists, like myself, do not avoid inquiring about suicidal thoughts in depressed teens for fear of creating more suicidal thoughts, because it's been shown to have the opposite effect.

And even if more knowledge DID lead to more sex, safer sex is arguably better than any unsafe sex.

Teaching children about healthy sexuality while they are still open to adult influence spares us from witnessing them putting themselves at risk later in life due to a lack of knowledge.

As adults, the thoughts of our children as sexual beings may make us uncomfortable, but the visuals of them tumbling down flights of stairs as toddlers spurned us to have safety conversations back then. The thoughts of them putting themselves through their own windshields motivates us to teach them how to navigate intersections and freeways.

If discussions about how to navigate their genitals is different, it is quite likely about our own level of discomfort with the subject – a poor reason to avoid the topic.

Teenagers are going to have sex, as they always have. This may or may not include your child, but most teens are physically adults, though not socially or emotionally. Biology often trumps social and religious mores. Fear, logic and even sometimes laws face similar fates.

Children and teens need to know that the safest sex of all is no sex, and we must help young people become self-confident enough to say "No" – despite peer and social pressures.

But they also have to know what "sex" is.

And they need to know what "safer sex" is.

Sooner or later, most of them do decide to become sexually active. They need to be prepared to protect themselves before they say, "Yes."

We can teach them to (and how to) protect themselves and get testing or treatment if they need it. We can teach them how to have fun, while being true to themselves and respectful of others.

The issue is not whether teens will get sex education. The issue is how and where will they gather information.

Young people are less likely to take sexual risks if they have:

- A positive view of sexuality

- Information that they need to take care of their sexual health

- Clarity about their own values and an understanding of their families' values

- Self-esteem and self-confidence

- Interpersonal skills, such as assertiveness and decision-making abilities

- An understanding of the consequences and results of both their actions and their inactions.

- A connection to home, family, and other caring adults in their community and school.

Chapter 49

WHAT UNDERAGERS NEED TO KNOW ABOUT SEX

- That sex is a part of one's personality – not the most interesting or most important part, but a part.

- That there are differences between sex, orientation, gender and identity.

- That no one needs to feel bad, scared, ashamed or unclean for being a sexual creature.

- That there are many healthy ways to think about and engage in sexual behavior.

- That there are many unhealthy ways to think about and engage in sexual behavior.

- That relationships are integral parts of healthy sexual behavior.

- That those relationships are formed in many different ways.

- That the most important relationship is their relationship with themselves.

- That sexual behavior and relationships have potential risks.

- That abstaining from sexual behavior is a choice.

- That engaging in sexual behavior is a choice.

- That it is important to take responsibility for one's sexual choices and behavior.

- How to make informed decisions and healthy choices

- How to take responsibility for one's sexual choices and behavior.

- That it is important to discuss their own feelings, have their own experiences and develop their own attitudes about sex.

- How media, social needs and pressure can impact sexual identity.

- How to create a positive self-image and identity in spite of these things.

- How to communicate about sex with potential partners.

- That it is important to know the names and definitions of sexual words, acts and safety measures.

- That humans are the only beings capable of consciously controlling their number of offspring.

- What is involved in the processes of conception, pregnancy and birth.

- That it is important to utilize birth control and safer sex every time they engage in sex activity.

- How to access and properly use birth control and safer sex methods.

- How to best avoid unwanted sexual experiences and consequences.

- The social, emotional, financial and physical consequences of failing to do practice safer sex, abiding by local laws or protecting themselves from negative sexual experiences.

- The laws in the region in which they live and potential legal ramifications of violating them.

- The resources available in case they need them.

Chapter 50

WHAT PARENTS NEED TO KNOW

There is a myth in this culture that this information needs to be shared in just the right way and at just the right time.

This commonly referred to as "The Talk."

But, it is not a Talk – it's Talks. As in, more than one.

As parents, we need to trust our judgment, our critical thinking and our teaching abilities – just like we do everything else.

We help them create boundaries, grow, reinforce their critical thinking skills and start conversations around values.

When we leave them to their own resources, we leave gaps to be filled by equally misinformed peers, pop culture or the school system.

The key to helping kids understand the basics about sex is:

To make it a part of regular conversation. It is not a one-time inoculation, it is a process.

- Find teachable moments and include sex whenever you talk about dating, love, drugs, friendship, health, media and other related subjects. Do it every chance you get. Bringing it up at the dinner table may not be a good idea, but song lyrics, websites, movies, newscasts, etc. can be excellent opportunities for the topics to come up.

- Keep the lines of communication open with your child. You'll need to discuss tough topics from time to time. If you and your teen are used to having conversations on a regular basis, even the awkward conversations will be easier. You don't want to think about them as sexually active creatures any more than they want to picture you as one. Sleep safe in the knowledge that even if your kids might be uncomfortable talking to you that they know they can.

- Respect your child's opinions. Enjoy the fact that your children are curious and have begun to inform their own opinions. Work to form a relationship with those opinions – even when they don't mesh with your own.

- If you cannot have the discussion with them, provide them with reliable/ responsible alternatives.

- Speak to your child's school about what they are teaching and the sexual education curriculum, and do not think that what your children are learning about sex outside your home is enough.

PART FIVE: OUTRO

Conclusion

I am writing this book with the intention of providing information, education and inspiration in order to contribute to healthy social and sexual relationships, as I understand them. I understand that not everyone will agree with my philosophy, though I hope (and believe) all of you reading this will find benefit from it.

As a parent myself, and someone who has worked with teens for almost twenty years, I want to help others understand that concepts such as pregnancy, sexual identity, pornography and even the word "sex" itself has a very different meaning than it did when I began this work. Nothing can be taken for granted – this book is just as much for you as it is for the teenagers in your life.

I encourage adults to use this book as a birthday, Valentine's or graduation gift for any young person in your life between the ages of fourteen and twenty. It would also be a useful and thoughtful gift to the parents of youth of those ages.

- This book can be left in an accessible place such as a bookshelf, desktop, coffee table or the waiting room of a health professional.

- Parents can write notes in the margins and quietly leave it on your underager's nightstand – inviting them to ask you questions.

- Therapists and teachers can use it as an educational guideline for groups.

- Parents can read it chapter-by-chapter with their sons, planning discussions afterward.

For the young people reading this, I encourage you to do the same. This book is designed to give you the tools and knowledge that you need to engage in sex and sexuality in a healthy way – having fun while doing as little harm to yourself or others as possible.

- Share the things you find in this book with friends and partners – in a "spread-info-not-Chlamydia" kind of vibe.

- Read and revisit it as you grow and change as a sexual person.

- This book can also be used to help you help encourage your parents have these talks with you as well – there is a section devoted exclusively to them. Dog-ear a few specific pages or underline a random section with a highlighter and leave it out for them to find. They'll come to you.

For everyone reading this, I value feedback, questions and strive to be available as needed. I can be reached via my website, Beheroes.net, and am available for speaking and educational engagements.

Disclaimer

This book is intended to provide information, education and inspiration. It is intended to be an adjunct to (not a substitute for) professional medical advice.

In addition, much of the information included here can and will most likely change with time and the rapid development of technology, science and culture.

It is important for anyone reading this book to continue to educate themselves and consult medical providers and professionals as well as other trusted sources (including and especially parents) around how any of the issues or information contained inside relates to their own situation, identity and personal growth.

I strongly encourage anyone reading this to seek adult support and professional help – especially if:

- You are just becoming sexually active
- Your sexual behavior is causing problems in your life
- Your sexual behavior is causing problems in others' lives
- You have (or might have) gotten someone pregnant
- You fear you have been exposed to infection
- You have a history of abuse
- You are afraid of your sexual or romantic partner

- You have a history of self-harm behaviors

- You have questions about your sexual identity

- You feel unsupported or actively bullied because of your sexual identity.

Glossary

- **ABORTION** – Ending the life of a developing fetus via a number of techniques.

- **ABSTINENCE** – Choosing to not participate in sex and sexual play with other people.

- **ADOLESCENCE** – The transition between childhood and adulthood.

- **AFTERPLAY** – All of the fun, lovey, gropey stuff you do after the ACTUAL sex.

- **ACQUIRED IMMUNE DEFICIENCY SYNDROME** – When a person's immune system is considered too compromised (too weak) to keep us safe from bacterial and viral infections that they would normally be able to fend off.

- **THE AGE RULE** – A formula to ensure that we engage in sexual/ romantic relationships with people within our general cohort.

- **AIDS** (see **ACQUIRED IMMUNE DEFICIENCY SYNDROME**)

- **ALTERNATIVES** – A natural, contraceptive/safer sex method involving the penetration of orifices other than the vagina – such as the mouth or anus.

- **ANAL SEX** – A man puts his penis into the anus of another man or a woman.

- **ANALINGUS** – Putting a mouth on someone's anus.

- **ANDROGYNY** – Having both traditionally masculine and feminine qualities, or qualities that do not fit cleanly into typical masculine and feminine roles.

- **ANUS** – The opening of the rectum, which is also highly sensitive to touch and can provide sexual pleasure.

- **BALLS** (see **TESTICLES**)

- **BEATING OFF** (see **MASTURBATION**)

- **THE BIG R** – Code for Relationship, Respect and/or Reciprocation in terms of sexual interaction.

- **BIOLOGY** – The physical make-up of the human body – its parts and functions.

- **BISEXUALITY** – Some degree of attraction to both sexes.

- **BLOW JOB** (see **FELLATIO**)

- **BLUE BALLS** – Localized pain in the testicles that can happen if blood flow to the penis (which makes it erect) lasts too long.

- **BODY IMAGE** – The way we see ourselves in our minds and mirrors, and the ways we feel about that.

- **BONER** (see **ERECTION**)

- **BONER SHAME** – Anxiety around the size of one's penis.

- **BOTTOM** – The person being penetrated during anal sex.

- **BREASTS** – Female body mammary glands, which secrete milk used to feed infants. They are sensitive to touch, and can enhance sexual pleasure.

- **BREAST SELF-EXAM** – Checking for lumps, bumps or changes in the breasts as a preventative screen for cancer.

- **CANDIDIASIS** (see **YEAST INFECTION**)

- **CERVICAL CAP** – A custom-fitted, thimble-shaped, latex cap, which covers the cervix and prevents the passage of sperm.

- **CERVICAL SHIELD** – A silicone cup attached to the cervix via suction, which covers the cervix, and prevents the passage of sperm.

- **CERVIX** – A small, doughnut-shaped organ, which connects the uterus and the back of the vagina.

- **CHLAMYDIA** – A bacterium which causes painful and burning discharges during urination and intercourse, inflammation of the rectum and cervix, swelling of the testicles, bleeding after sex and, eventually, sterility.

- **CIRCUMSCISION** – A controversial surgical procedure in which the foreskin is cut off or removed from a penis.

- **CHANCROID** – Sexually transmitted bacterium in the form of a small, pus filled, and painful ulcers on the genitals.

- **CLITORIS** – A short shaft with a very sensitive tip, the only female organ whose sole purpose is pleasure, and it plays an incredibly important part of arousal for women.

- **CLOSETED** – The opposite out being out as a gay person.

- **COCK** (see **PENIS**)

- **COME** (see **SEMEN**)

- **COMING** (see **EJACULATION**)

- **COMING OUT** – The process of accepting and being open about one's sexual orientation and gender identity.

- **CONDOMS (FEMALE)** – Longer, wider form of male condoms, inserted into the vagina or rectum and held in place with bendable rings at both ends.

- **CONDOMS (MALE)** – Latex coverings placed on the penis to prevent sperm from entering the vagina, anus or mouth.

- **CONSENT** – On-purpose, sober, chosen, informed, mutual, honest, and obvious agreement.

- **CONTRACEPTIVES** – reduce the likelihood of pregnancy.

- **CONVERSION THERAPY** – Ineffective and harmful use of prayer, counseling and sometimes drugs or shock therapy meant to "cure" gay people.

- **CRABS** – Tiny, grey bugs that attach to your skin, turn darker when swollen with blood, and attach eggs to your pubic hair.

- **CROSS-DRESSER** (see **TRANSVESTITE**)

- **CUM** (see **SEMEN**)

- **CUMMING** (see **EJACULATION**)

- **CUNNILINGUS** – Oral sex on a woman

- **DATE RAPE DRUGS** – Chemicals usually put into someone's drink, which weaken you and impair your ability to move or remember things.

- **DEATH GRIP** – Masturbating too quickly and/or with a very tight grip.

- **DENTAL DAMS** – Ultra-thin, often scented, latex sheets placed over the vulva or anus during oral sex.

- **DEPO-PROVERA** – A once-per-three-months birth control injection.

- **DESIRE** – Interest in sex and sexual behavior /feeling attracted to someone.

- **DIAPHRAGM** – A shallow rubber cup, which covers the cervix to prevent the passage of sperm.

- **DICK** (see **PENIS**)

- **DRAG KING** – Females who live part-time as members of the other sex, primarily as performers – singing and/or dancing.

- **DRAG QUEEN** – Males live part-time as members of the other sex, primarily as performers – singing and/or dancing.

- **DRY SEX** (see **OUTERCOURSE**)

- **DYKE** – Offensive term for lesbians.

- **EATING HER OUT** (see **CUNNILINGUS**)

- **ECP's** (see **EMERGENCY CONTRACEPTION PILLS**)

- **EMERGENCY CONTRACEPTION PILLS** – Increased doses of birth control hormones used by some as a back-up when other means of contraception have failed.

- **EGGS** – Contain the female DNA and twenty-three chromosomes, which (if joined by the DNA and chromosomes of a sperm) create an embryo.

- **EJACULATION** – The discharge of fluids usually during orgasm.

- **EMBRYO** – A human organism in the early stages of development (typically conception through the eight week).

- **ERECTION** – A penis engorged with blood and "hard".

- **EROGENOUS ZONES** – Areas which, when stimulated, can lead to high levels of sexual arousal and powerful orgasms.

- **ESSURE** – Small, (non-surgical) metallic implants called inserted into the fallopian tubes to block pregnancy.

- **EXCITEMENT** – Feeling actively turned on or engaged in sexual activity.

- **FAG/FAGGOT** – Offensive term for gay males.

- **FALLOPIAN TUBES** (also known as oviducts) **?**– Lead the egg from the ovaries into the uterus after ovulation (the release of the egg). Often, eggs are fertilized here.

- **FAM's** (see **FERTILITY AWARENESS METHODS**)

- **FELLATIO** – Oral sex on a guy.

- **FERTILITY AWARENESS METHODS** (see **RHYTHM METHODS**).

- **FERTILIZATION** – The fusion of the sperm and egg.

- **FETUS** – A human organism after eight weeks of development, when recognizable human characteristics begin to show.

- **FLACCID** – A penis when it is not erect or "hard".

- **FOREPLAY** – All the fun, lovey, gropey stuff you do before the ACTUAL sex.

- **FORESKIN** – A retractable, double-layered, fold of skin that covers and protects the glans of the penis when it is not erect

- **FRENCH KISSING** – Opening the mouth and putting your tongue in the other person's mouth (or letting them do that to yours).

- **FRENULUM** – The sensitive area under the head of the penis.

- **GARDASIL** – A vaccine that prevents the types of Human Papilloma Viruses (HPV), which can cause cervical cancer and genital warts.

- **GAY** – A male who is attracted to another male.

- **GENDER** – A social phenomenon, often used to refer to ways that people act, interact, or feel about themselves, which are associated with boys/men and girls/women. This refers to how "guy-like" or "chick-like" one is.

- **GENDER QUEER** – Being a third sex-both male AND female and/or falling completely outside the gender binary as genderless – being neither male nor female.

- **GENITALS** – Reproductive body parts.

- **GENITAL WARTS** (see **HPV**).

- **GONORRHEA** – A bacterium, which causes sterility, arthritis, heart problems, and a pus-like discharge from the urethra, which causes pain during urination.

- **GLANS** – The sensitive "head" of the penis.

- **GRAFENBERG SPOT** – A female erogenous zone located inside the vagina.

- **GROWER** – A shorter, soft penis that increases, sometime doubling or tripling in length, as it gets erect.

- **G-SPOT** (see **GRAFENBERG SPOT**).

- **GYNE** (see **VAGINA**).

- **HARD-ON** (see **ERECTION**)

- **HEPATITIS B** – A very contagious virus, which attacks the liver, leading to yellow skin, brown urine cirrhosis, cancer and possibly death.

- **HERMAPHRODITE** – A stigmatizing word for intersexed persons, which should not be used to refer to people.

- **HERPES SIMPLEX 1** – Cold sores or fever blisters around the mouth.

- **HERPES SIMPLEX 2** – Hot, itchy blisters, which burst open and create ulcers around the genital areas.

- **HETEROSEXUAL** – Romantic or sexual attraction to someone of the opposite sex.

- **HICKEYS** – Bruises caused by sucking blood to the surface of the skin.

- **HIV** (see **HUMAN IMMUNODEFICIENCY VIRUS**)

- **HUMAN IMMUNODEFICIENCY VIRUS** – A viral STI, which slowly weakens your immune system – your body's mechanism for fighting off infections.

- **HOMOPHOBIA** – Discrimination and fear against gay people.

- **HOMOSEXUAL** – Romantic or sexual attraction to someone of the same sex.

- **HORNY** (see **DESIRE**).

- **HPV** (see **HUMAN PAPILLOMA VIRUS**)

- **HSV** (see **HERPES**)

- **HUMAN PAPILLOMA VIRUS** – Cell-mutating Viruses that cause a variety of itchy, flesh-colored, cauliflower-like warts, some of which also contribute to cancers in the cervix, vulva and penis.

- **HVB** (see **HEPATITIS VIRUS B**)

- **HYMEN** – A thin, piece of tissue that partially covers the opening of the vagina.

- **IDENTITY** – The who or what someone is or wishes to be known as.

- **INDULGENCE** – The decision whether or not to remain abstinent.

- **INTERSEX** – A person having biological characteristics of both the male and female sexes or who is chromosomally (internally) one sex, while physically (externally) another.

- **INTRAUTERINE DEVICE** – A small, plastic, T-shaped device inserted into the woman's uterus containing copper, which helps prevent the fertilization and implantation of eggs.

- **INTRAUTERINE SYSTEM** – A small, plastic, T-shaped device inserted into the woman's uterus containing hormones, which help prevent the fertilization and implantation of eggs.

- **IUD** (see **INTRAUTERINE DEVICE**)

- **IUS** (see **INTRAUTERINE SYSTEM**)

- **JACKING OFF** (see **MASTURBATION**).

- **JERKING OFF** (see **MASTURBATION**).

- **JILLING OFF** (see **MASTURBATION**).

- **KINSEY SCALE** – A questionnaire in the form of a continuum that served to rate a person's attraction and behavior with regard to sex.

- **KISSING** – Touching lips with someone else's as an expression of love or desire.

- **LABIA MAJORA** – An outer layer of lips, which cover and protect the vagina.

- **LABIA MINORA** – An inner layer of lips, which cover and protect the vagina.

- **LEA'S SHIELD** (see **CERVICAL SHIELD**)

- **LESBIAN** – A female who is attracted to another female.

- **LUBRICATION** – A substance designed or created to reduce friction.

- **LUNELLE** – A once-per-month birth control shot.

- **MANUAL SEX** (see **MASTURBATION**).

- **MASTURBATION** – Sexual stimulation or rubbing (usually) of one's own genitals, to achieve sexual arousal – usually to the point of orgasm.

- **MENSTRUATION** – The shedding of blood and membrane, which would have formed the nourishing home for an embryo to grow into a fetus.

- **MIFEPREX** (see **MIFEPRISTONE**).

- **MIFEPRISTONE** – Chemical abortion drug, which induces abortion in the forts forty-nine days of gestation.

- **MIRENA** (see **INTRAUTERINE SYSTEM**).

- **MISSIONARY POSITION** – A heterosexual sex position in which both partners face one another.

- **MONOGAMY** – Having sex with only one other person, within a committed long-term relationship, and with someone who has tested free of any STI's.

- **MONS** – The fatty tissue above a woman's pubic bone – the part usually covered with hair.

- **MORNING AFTER PILL** – A misnomer for Emergency Contraception.

- **NEGATIVE BODY IMAGE** – A perception of ourselves that may not be true or that causes shame, anxiety or self-consciousness.

- **NOCTURNAL EMISSIONS** (see **WET DREAMS**).

- **NONOXYNOL-9** – The most popular spermicide in America. It kills both sperm and HIV, but it also causes irritation to the internal vaginal and anal walls.

- **NON-MARITAL SEX** – Having sex outside of marriage.

- **NUVA-RING** (see **VAGINAL RING**).

- **ORAL SEX** – When one person puts their mouth or tongue on the genitals of another.

- **ORGASM** – The point at which sexual tension is released, creating waves of pleasurable sensations as well as muscular contractions of the penis (male) or vagina (female) and anus (both), which eventually end in intense feelings, often accompanied by ejaculation.

- **ORIENTATION** – What sex you choose to be sexual with and its relationship to your own (whether you are gay, straight or bisexual).

- **ORTHO-EVRA** (see **THE PATCH**).

- **OUTERCOURSE** – Sex with clothes on and/or that avoids penetration of any kind.

- **OVARIES** – Ovum (or egg) producing, reproductive organs in females.

- **OVULATION** – The release of the egg.

- **THE PATCH** – A slow-releasing, hormonal patch, which prevents fertilization and implantation of eggs.

- **PENIS** – The reproductive organ, for male animals.

- **PELVIC INFLAMMATORY DISEASE** – A serious infection (usually the result of a sexually transmitted infection such as Chlamydia or Gonorrhea), which spreads from the vagina and cervix into the reproductive organ.

- **PERIOD** (see **MENSTRUATION**)

- **PEGGING** – A man being anally penetrated in some way by a female partner.

- **PERSONAL SAFETY** – Things you can do ahead of time to keep yourself safe and lessen the chances of being victimized.

- **PID** (see **PELVIC INFLAMMATORY DISEASE**)

- **THE PILL** – A daily pill of estrogen and/ or progestin hormones, which is taken once a day to prevent the eggs from releasing, help thicken cervical mucus and/ or prevent fertilized eggs from implanting in the uterus.

- **PIV** – Penis-In-Vagina sex.

- **PLAN B** (see **EMERGENCY CONTRACEPTION**).

- **POSITIVE** (see POZ).

- **POSITIVE BODY IMAGE** – An acceptance of the unique qualities of our own bodies and a feeling of comfort and confidence with them.

- **POST-EXPOSURE PROPHYLAXES** – A month-long medication regimen, which greatly decreases the likelihood of HIV infection if taken within the first seventy-two hours of exposure.

- **PORNOGRAPHY** – Media designed to sexually excite people.

- **POZ** – A term, particularly in the gay community, for people who are HIV-Positive.

- **PRE-CUM** – Lubricating fluid released from the tip of a penis during arousal.

- **PREMARITAL SEX** – A misnomer for sex prior to marriage. As marriage is not currently available to everyone, a more accurate term is non-marital sex.

- **PREMATURE EJACULATION** – Ejaculating very quickly or much more quickly than your partner.

- **PREMENSTRUAL SYNDROME (PMS)** – A range of (typically negative) symptoms and effects that happen during the period between ovulation and menstruation.

- **PROSTATE GLAND** – One of the glands that help create seminal fluid. The prostate is also called the "male G-Spot," and is considered a male erogenous zone.

- **PUBERTY** – The process which begins adolescence.

- **PUBIC LICE** (see **CRABS**).

- **PUSSY** (see **VAGINA**).

- **QUEER** – A sexual identity on the continuum other than of straight.

- **RAPE CULTURE** – Judgments and cultural biases about women being targets of hostility, violence or viewed as less-than, as property or as only-there-for-sex.

- **REFRACTORY PERIOD** – The time between when someone has an orgasm before they can have another one.

- **REPARATIVE THERAPY** – Ineffective and harmful use of prayer, counseling and sometimes drugs or shock therapy to "cure" gay people.

- **RIMMING** (see **ANALINGUS**)

- **ROPHYS/ ROOFIES** – Date rape drugs.

- **RHYTHM METHODS** – A natural contraceptive method which involves charting of the menstrual cycles in order to predict approximately nine "unsafe" days in which one does not have intercourse.

- **RU-486** – A previous name for Mifeprex/ Mifepristone – a chemical abortion drug.

- **SADDLEBACKING** – Participating in oral and anal sex to mistakenly preserve virginity.

- **SAFE SEX** – A misnomer, which generally refers to Abstinence, Monogamy or Masturbation.

- **SAFER SEX** – Techniques, which deal with the reduction of exposure to disease.

- **SCABIES** (see **CRABS**).

- **SCROTUM** – The sac of skin and muscle, which contains and (theoretically) protects the testicles.

- **SEASONALE** – A twelve-month regimen of birth control pills, which reduces periods to approximately four per year.

- **SELF-ESTEEM** – The ways in which one considers or feels about themselves as a person.

- **SEMEN** – The milky combination of sperm and other liquids gathered along the way. Also called "come" or "cum."

- **SHOWER** – A long, soft penis that does not increase much in length as it becomes erect.

- **SEX** – One's physical parts and biological status as male or female.

- **SEXTING** – Sending graphic images and pornographic videos via text message to friends – considered child pornography if under eighteen.

- **SEXUAL ABUSE** – Direct touching, fondling and intercourse, against a person's will.

- **SEXUAL ASSAULT** – Unwanted sexual contact or threats, such as rape.

- **SEXUAL HARASSMENT** – Unwelcome attention of a sexual nature.

- **THE SHOT** – An injection of hormones, which prevent the releasing and joining of eggs as well as the implantation of fertilized eggs.

- **SLUT** – A shaming term for a sexualized female, considered unfair because there is no male equivalent.

- **SMEGMA** – Comprised of bacteria, yeasts, stale urine and dead skin cells which can collect under the foreskin of uncircumcised males to form a white, cheesy substance.

- **SPERM** – The male reproductive cells, comprised of twenty-three chromosomes, which (if joined by the DNA and chromosomes of an egg) create an embryo.

- **SPERMICIDE** – A foam, cream, jelly, film suppository or tablet placed inside the vagina, which kills and blocks sperm from entering the vaginal canal.

- **THE SPONGE** – A soft, disc-shaped device made of polyurethane foam, which contains spermicide, placed inside the vagina prior to sex.

- **STD's** (see **SEXUALLY TRANSMITTED DISEASES**)

- **SEXUALLY TRANSMITTED DISEASES** – Organisms, syndromes and Infections that are spread through sexual contact. (see **STI's**).

- **STI's** (see **SEXUALLY TRANSMITTED INFECTIONS**)

- **SEXUALLY TRANSMITTED INFECTIONS** – Organisms, syndromes and Infections that are spread through sexual contact.

- **STERILIZATION** (see **VASECTOMY** or **TUBAL LIGATION**).

- **STRAIGHT** (see **HETEROSEXUAL**).

- **SYPHILIS** – A bacterial infection causing a series of symptoms including, crater-like sores a painful rash and death.

- **T CELLS** – One specific type of blood cell that helps defend against infections and diseases.

- **TESTICLES** – Two small organs, which produce the male hormone, (testosterone) and make sperm.

- **Testosterone** – The primary male hormone produced in the testicles.

- **TOP** – The person being penetrating during anal sex.

- **TRANSGENDER** – An umbrella term used to describe people whose gender identity (sense of themselves as male or female) or gender expression may differ from the parts they were born with.

- **TRANNSEXUALS** – Transgender people who live or wish to live as members of the gender opposite to the sex they were born with.

- **TRANSVESTITES** – (Typically straight) People who wear the clothing of the opposite sex.

- **TRICHOMONIASIS** – A parasite, which causes irritation inside the penis, discharge with a strong odor, or a slight burning after urination and ejaculation.

- **TUBAL LIGATION** – Surgically severing the tubes, in which the sperm and egg meet in women to block pregnancy.

- **URETHRA** – The passage through the penis or vagina and opens to the outside to pass urine from the body.

- **URETHRITIS** – Inflammation caused by small amounts of bacteria or yeast in the vagina or urethra, which grow more than normal.

- **UTERUS** – The womb in which the embryo attaches and eventually grows into a fetus.

- **URINARY TRACT INFECTIONS** (or **UTI's**) – Bacterial infection of the urethra.

- **VAG/ VADGE** (see **VAGINA**)

- **VAGINA** – The reproductive organ for female mammals. It is also called a birth canal.

- **VAGINAL RING** – A combination of the pill and cervical cap in the form of a bendable, two-inch plastic ring worn around the cervix for three weeks each month.

- **VAGINITIS** – Inflammation caused by small amounts of bacteria or yeast in the vagina, which grow more than normal.

- **VAS DEFRENS** – The transport passageway of sperm to the urethra in males.

- **VASECTOMY** – Surgically severing the tubes, which carry sperm in men, to block pregnancy.

- **VD** (see **VENEREAL DISEASE**)

- **VIRGINITY** – The state of sexual inexperience.

- **VENEREAL DISEASE** (see **STI's**).

- **WET DREAM** – A buildup of sperm spontaneously ejaculated while a guy is sleeping.

- **WHORE** (see **SLUT**).

- **YEAST INFECTION** – A fungal infection of the vagina.

Resources

ASSAULT AND ABUSE

WEB

National Youth Violence Prevention Center
Safeyouth.org

BOOK

The Anger Workbook
by Frank B. Minirth and Les Carter

The Gift of Fear
by Gavin DeBecker

Victims No Longer: Men Recovering from Incest and Other Sexual Child Abuse
by Mike Lew

Wounded Boys, Heroic Men: A Man's Guide to Recovering from Child Abuse
by Daniel Jay Sonkin and Lenore E. A. Walker.

PHONE

Gay and Transgender Hate Crime Hotline
1-800-616-HATE

Homeless/ Runaway National Runaway Hotline
1-800-231-6946

National Domestic Violence Hotline
1-800-799-7233

National Youth Crisis Hotline
1-800-442-HOPE

Rape, Abuse, Incest National Network
1-800-656-HOPE

Stop it Now!
1-888-773-8368

Teen Helpline
1-800-400-0900

GLBTQ

WEB

American Psychological Association
Apa.org

Parents and Friends of Lesbians and Gays
Pflag.org

Gay Lesbian and Straight Education Network
GLSEN.org
Gayteenresources.org

GLAAD: The Gay and Lesbian Alliance Against Defamation
Glad.org

HRC: The Human Rights Campaign
Hrc.org

The Intersex Society of North America
Isna.org

The It Gets Better Project
ItGetsBetter.org

Lambda Legal Defense and Educational Fund
Lambdalegal.org

OutProud
Outproud.com

Tolerance.org

BOOKS

GLBTQ: The Survival Guide for Queer and Questioning Teens
By Kelly Huegel

Always My Child: A Parents' Guide to Understanding Your Gay, Lesbian, Bisexual, Transgendered or Questioning Son or Daughter
By Kevin Jennings and Pat Shapiro

Boyfriend 101: A Gay Guy's Guide to Dating, Romance and Finding True Love
By Jim Sullivan

HEALTH AND HARM

WEB

Anorexia Nervosa and Related Eating Disorders
ANRED.COM

Makelovenotporn.com

Through The Flame
Throughtheflame.org

BOOKS

In the Shadows of the Net
Patrick Carnes, David Delmonico and Elizabeth Griffin

My Body My Self for Boys
Lynda Madaras

Real Boys: Rescuing Our Sons From the Myths of Boyhood.
William Pollack

The Wonder of Boys
Michael Gurian

PHONE

Drug Help National Helplines
1-800-378-4435

National Suicide Prevention Hotline
1-800-273-TALK

Eating Disorders Awareness and Prevention
1-800-931-2237

Eating Disorders Center
1-888-236-1188

Teenline
1-800-522-TEEN

Center for the Prevention of School Violence
1-800-299-6504

Gay, Lesbian, Bisexual and Transgender (GLBT) Youth
1-800-850-8078

Gay Men's Domestic Violence
1-800-832-1901

Gay and Transgender Hate Crime Hotline
1-800-616-HATE

National Adolescent Suicide Hotline
1-800-621-4000

The Trevor Project
1-866-488-7386

PREGNANCY

WEB

American Social Health Association
Iwannaknow.com

condomania.com

Momdadimpregnant.com

National Abortion Federation
prochoice.org

National Campaign to Prevent Teen Pregnancy
Teenpregnancy.org

National Right To Life
nrlc.org

Planned Parenthood
Plannedparenthood.org

PHONE

Emergency Contraception Information
1-888-NOT 2 LATE

National Abortion Federation Hotline
1-800-772-9100

Planned Parenthood
1-800-230-PLAN

Pregnancy Helpline
1-800-848-5683

SEXUALITY

WEB

About.com

Advocatesforyouth.org

Goaskalice.com

The Guttmacher Institute
Guttmacher.org

The Kaiser Foundation
Kff.org

The Kinsey Institute
www.iub.edu

KidsHealth
kidshealth.org

MakeLoveNotPorn.com

Scarletteen.org

Sexedbootcamp.com

Sexuality Information Council of Teens
Siecus.org

Talkwithyourkids.org

Teachingsexualhealth.ca

Teenadvice.about.com

BOOKS

Birds + Bees + YOUR kids—A Guide to Sharing Your Beliefs About Sexuality, Love and Relationships
By Amy Lang

The Guide To Getting It On
By Paul Joannides

Our Bodies Ourselves (teen version)
By Ruth Bell Alexander

What's Happening to My Body
By Madaras and Anderson

S.E.X.
By Heather Corinna

PHONE

Teen Helpline
1-800-400-0900

Teenline
1-800-522-TEEN

STI'S

WEB

Centers for Disease Control and Prevention
cdc.gov

Kidshealth.org

Planned Parenthood
plannedparenthood.org

Teenwire.com

PHONE

HIV/STD hotline
1-800-678-1595

National Youth Crisis Hotline
1-800-442-HOPE

Planned Parenthood
1-800-230-PLAN

Teen Helpline
1-800-400-0900

Teenline
1-800-522-TEEN

References
(Endnotes)

INTRODUCTION

1   Facts on American Teens' Sexual and Reproductive Health. Guttmacher Institute. http://www.guttmacher.org/pubs/FB-ATSRH.html#n25.   (Accessed   September 2008).

2   Kaiser Family Foundation. 2005. U.S. Teen Sexual Activity. Kff.org. http://www.kff.org/youthhivstds/upload/U-S-Teen-Sexual-Activity-Fact-Sheet.pdf.   (Accessed January 2011).

3   Ibid.

4   Internet Crimes Against Children. 2001. Youth Internet Safety Survey. http://www.ojp.usdoj.gov/ovc/publications/bulletins/internet_2_2001/internet_2_01_6.html. (Accessed July 2011).

5   The National Campaign To Prevent Teen and Unplanned Pregnancy. 2008. Sex and Tech: Results From a Survey of Teens and Young Adults. Thenationalcampaign. org.   http://www.thenationalcampaign.org/sextech/PDF/SexTech_Summary.pdf. (Accessed August 2011).

6   American National Standard Safe Practices for Motor Vehicle Operation, American Society of Safety Engineers, Des Plaines, IL, 2006

Chapter 3: PUBERTY

7   KidsHealth. Boys and Puberty. http://kidshealth.org/kid/grow/boy/boys_puberty. html. (Accessed June 2011).

8   Planned Parenthood. Puberty 101 for Parents. http://www.plannedparenthood.org/ parents/puberty-101-parents-22999.htm (Accessed February 2011)

Chapter 4: OTHER BODY ISSUES

9   Planned Parenthood. Puberty 101 for Parents. http://www.plannedparenthood.org/ parents/puberty-101-parents-22999.htm (Accessed March 2011)

10   Songhai Barcligt, M.D. (2010) Womenshealth.gov. Premenstrual syndrome (PMS) Fact Sheet. http://www.womenshealth.gov/publications/our-publications/fact-sheet/premenstrual-syndrome.cfm (Accessed July 2011).

11   Curtains for Semi-Nude Justice Statue. Tuesday 29. January 2002. http://news. bbc.co.uk/2/hi/1788845.stm. (Accessed May 2011).

12   Mike Zimmerman. (2011). 15 Facts You Didn't Know About Your Penis. Men'sHealth.com http://www.menshealth.com/mhlists/penis_facts/Penis_Fact_9. php. (Accessed July, 2011).

13   Paul Gebhard and Alan Johnson. (1979/1998). *The Kinsey Data: Marginal Tabulations of the 1938-1963 Interviews Conducted by the Institute for Sex Research (reprint edition).* Bloomington, IN: Indiana University Press.

14   "Alice" (a team of Columbia University health educators, health care providers, and other health professionals, along with a staff of information and research specialists and writers. Team members have advanced degrees in public health, health education, medicine, and counseling). (2002). How deep is the average vagina, and does it elongate when something's in it? Goaskalice!..Columbia.edu. http://www.goaskalice.columbia.edu/2067.html (Accessed August 2011).

15   K. Paige (May 1978). "The Ritual of Circumcision". *Human Nature*: 40 – 8.

16   Carrie McLaren. (1997). Porn Flakes: Kellogg, Graham and the Crusade for Moral Fiber. Stay Free! Magazine.org. http://www.stayfreemagazine.org/10/graham.htm. (Accessed December 2010).

17   Doctors opposing Circumcision. (2008). The Use of Male Circumcision to Prevent HIV Infection. http://www.doctorsopposingcircumcision.org/info/HIVStatement. html. (Accessed March 2011).

18   Clearinghouse of Male Circumcision for HIV Prevention. (2008). Observational Research on Male Circumcision. http://www.malecircumcision.org/research/ observational_research.html (Accessed March 2011).

19   Doctors opposing Circumcision. (2008). The Use of Male Circumcision to Prevent HIV Infection. http://www.doctorsopposingcircumcision.org/info/HIVStatement. html. (Accessed March 2011).

20   J. Steven Svoboda. (2010). CDC: US Circumcision Rate Has Plunged to 33%. Men's News Daily. http://mensnewsdaily.com/2010/08/17/cdc-us-circumcision-rate-has-plunged-to-33/. (Accessed August 2010).

21   Dave, Johnson, Fenton, Mercer, Erens, Wellings. (2003). Male circumcision in Britain: findings from a national probability sample survey. Sex Transm Infect 79: 499-500.

Chapter 5: BODY IMAGE

22   Nicole Hawkinhs, Ph.D. Battling Our Bodies? Understanding and Overcoming Negative Body Images. Eating Disorder rReferral and Information Center.http:// www.edreferral.com/body_image.htm. (Accessed May 2011).

23   Kate Fox. 1997. Mirror, mirror – *A summary of research findings on body image.* Social Issues Research Centre. http://www.sirc.org/publik/mirror.html. (Accessed 2011).

24   South Carolina Department of Mental Health. 2006. Eating Disorder Statistics. http://www.state.sc.us/dmh/anorexia/statistics.htm. (Accessed February 2011).

25   South Carolina Department of Mental Health. Eating Disorder Statistics. http:// www.state.sc.us/dmh/anorexia/statistics.htm. (Accessed May 2011).

26   South Carolina Department of Mental Health. Eating Disorder Statistics. http:// www.state.sc.us/dmh/anorexia/statistics.htm. (Accessed May 2011).

27   B.A. Robinson. 2006.   REPARATIVE THERAPY: STATEMENTS BY PROFESSIONAL ASSOCIATIONS AND THEIR LEADERS. Religious Tolerance. org. (Accessed June 2011) page 33

SECTION II - IDENTITY

Chapter 8: HOMOSEXUALITY

28   News-Medcial.Net. 2006. "1,500 Animal Species Practice Homosexuality". http:// www.news-medical.net/news/2006/10/23/20718.aspx.   (Accessed September, 2011).

29   Adherents.com. 2007. Composite U.S. Demographics. http://www.adherents.com/ adh_dem.html (Accessed July, 2011).

Chapter 9: BISEXUALITY AND THE CONTINUUM

30   The Kinsey Institute. 2009. Kinsey's Heterosexual-Homosexual Rating Scale. http://www.iub.edu/~kinsey/research/ak-hhscale.html.   (Accessed September 2011).

31   Biology News Net. 2008. Homosexual Behavior Due to Genetics and Environmental Factors. http://www.biologynews.net/archives/2008/06/29/homosexual_behavior_ due_to_genetics_and_environmental_factors.html. (Accessed June 2011).

32   Frankowski BL. 2004. American Academy of Pediatrics Committee on Adolescence: Sexual Orientation and Adolescents. *Pediatrics* 113 (6):1827-32.

33   Lambda.org. 1994. Be Yourself: Questions and Answers for Gay, Lesbian and Bisexual Youth. http://www.lambda.org/be_yourself.htm. (Accessed May 2011).

34   Parents and Friends of Lesbians and Gays. 2008. Gay, Lesbian, Bisexual, and Transgender (GLBT) Rights Fact Sheet. PFLAG.org. http://community.pflag.org/ page.aspx?pid=442. (Accessed June 2011).

35   Remafedi, Farrow and Deisher. (1991). Risk Factors for Attempted Suicide in Gay and Bisexual Youth. Pediatrics, 87, pp. 869 – 875.

36   R.L. Spitzer. 1981. The Diagnositic Status of Homosexuality in DSM-III: A Reformulation of the Issues. American Journal of Psychiatry 138:210-215.

37   Human Rights Campaign. 2009. Matthew Shepard and James Byrd, Jr. Hate Crimes Prevention Act. Hrc.org. http://www.hrc.org/issues/5660.htm. (Accessed November 2011).

38   American Psychiatric Association Assembly. 2000. Therapies Focused on Attempts to Change Sexual Orientation (Reparative or Conversion Therapies) POSITION STATEMENT. American Psychiatric Association. http://www.psych.org/Departments/EDU/Library/APAOfficialDocumentsandRelated/PositionStatements/200001.aspx. (Accessed August 2011).

SECTION IV - SEXUAL ACTIVITY

Chapter 13: SEXUAL AROUSAL

39   Adapted from Masters and Johnson. 1981 (1st ed. 1966). *Human Sexual Response*, New York: Bantam.

40   Dan Savage. 2007. Savage Love: Play With Her Clit. The Stranger, July 19, 2007.

41   Franklin Lowe, M.D., M.P.H., F.A.C.S. 2006. All About Semen.The National Men's Resource Center. http://www.menstuff.org/issues/byissue/semen.html. (Accessed July 2011).

Chapter 14: SEXUAL ACTIVITY

42   Human Sexual Behavior. The Journal of Evolutionary Philosophy. http://www.evolutionary-philosophy.net/human_sexuality.html (Accessed August 2011).

Chapter 15: MASTURBATION

43   Gerressu, Mercer, Graham, Wellings, Johnson. (April 2008). "Prevalence of masturbation and associated factors in a British national probability survey". *Arch Sex Behav* 37 (2): 266 – 78.

44   Janus and Janus. *The Janus Report on Sexual Behavior*. 1993. New York: John Wiley and Sons.

45   Edwin Haeberle, Ph.D. 1983. *The Sex Atlas*. New York: The Continuum Publishing Company.

46   "Alice" (a team of Columbia University health educators, health care providers, and other health professionals, along with a staff of information and research specialists and writers. Team members have advanced degrees in public health, health education, medicine, and counseling). (1995). Masturbation Healthy? Goaskalice!.Columbia.edu.   http://www.goaskalice.columbia.edu/0539.html. (Accessed February 2011).

47   Justice Potter Stewart, concurring opinion in *Jacobellis v. Ohio* 378 U.S. 184 (1964).

48   *Jerry Ropelato*. 2006. Internet Pornography Statistics.Toptenreviews.com. http://internet-filter-review.toptenreviews.com/internet-pornography-statistics.html. (Accessed August 2011).

49   Jonathan Liew. 2009. All Men Watch porn, Scientists Find. The Telegraph. http://www.telegraph.co.uk/relationships/6709646/All-men-watch-porn-scientists-find.html. (Accessed December 2011).

Chapter 16: KISSING

50   William Case. 1995. *The Art of Kissing*. 2nd ed. New York, NY: St. Martin's Griffin.

Chapter 19: PIV

51   Güntürkün, O.Adult persistence of head-turning asymmetry. Nature, 421, 711, (2003).

52   The Medical Center for Female Sexuality. 2011. Female Orgasm. Centerforfemalesexuality.com. http://www.centerforfemalesexuality.com/orgasm.htm. (Accessed April 2011).

Chapter 20: ANAL SEX

53   Dan Savage. 2010. Wiggle Room. The Stranger – Savage Love. February 25, 2010.

54   Em and Lo. 2006. The Bottom Line. *New York Magazine* December, 2006.

55   Medcial News Today. 2008. Increase In Anal Intercourse Involving At-Risk Teens And Young Adults. Medicalnewstoday.com. http://www.medicalnewstoday.com/releases/130181.php. (Accessed January 2011).

56   Dan Savage. 2009. Saddlebacked! The Stranger: Savage Love. January 29, 2009.

57   Bill Brent. 2002. The Ultimate Guide to Anal Sex for Men. San franciso: Cleis Press.

58   Divisions of HIV/AIDS Prevention. 2010. HIV Transmission.   National Center for HIV/AIDS, Viral Hepatitis, STD, and TB Prevention. http://www.cdc.gov/hiv/resources/qa/transmission.htm. (Accessed March 2011).

59   William Saletan. Posted Tuesday, Sept. 20, 2005. Ass Backwards: The media's silence about rampant anal sex. Slate.com.   http://www.slate.com/id/2126643/ (Accessed XXX).

60   Heather Boonstra. 2005. Condoms, Contraceptives and Nonoxynol-9: Complex Issues Obscured by Ideology. The Guttmacher Report on Public Policy 8: (2).

SECTION V - CHOICE MAKING/DECISION MAKING

Chapter 21: REGARDING ABSTINENCE

61   Harvard School of Public Health Press Releases. 2006. "Virginity Pledges" by Adolescents May Bias Their Reports of Premarital Sex. Harvard.edu. http://www.hsph.harvard.edu/news/press-releases/2006-releases/press05022006.html. (Accessed June 2011).

62   Planned Parenthood (adapted from World Health Organization 2007). Comparing effectiveness of birth control methods. Plannedparenthood.org. http://www.plannedparenthood.org/health-topics/birth-control/birth-control-effectiveness-chart-22710.htm. (Accessed December 2010).

SECTION VII - RISK REDUCTION

Chapter 26: SEXUALLY TRANSMITTED INFECTIONS (STI's)

63   Planned Parenthood. 2011. Sexually Transmitted Diseases (STDs). http://www.plannedparenthood.org/health-topics/stds-hiv-safer-sex-101.htm. (Accessed June 2011).

64   Minnesota Department of Health. 2011. STD Awareness Month Facts. health.state.mn.us.   http://www.health.state.mn.us/divs/idepc/dtopics/stds/stdmonth/stdmonthfacts.html. (Accessed April 2011).

65   American Social Health Association/Kaiser Family Foundation. 1998. STDs in America: How Many Cases and at What Cost? KFF.org. http://www.kff.org/womenshealth/1445-std_rep.cfm. (Accessed April 2011).

66   Do Something. 11 Facts About Teens and STIs. Dosomething.org. http://www.dosomething.org/tipsandtools/11-facts-about-teens-and-stds.   (Accessed June 2011).

67   Centers for Disease Control and Prevention. 2010. STDs in Adolescents and Young Adults. Dcd.gov. http://www.cdc.gov/std/stats09/adol.htm. (Accessed December 2010).

Chapter 27: STI PRIMER

68   New York State Department of Health. 2006. Gonorrhea Gonococcal Infection. Helath.ny.gov. http://www.health.ny.gov/diseases/communicable/gonorrhea/fact_sheet.htm. (Accessed November 2010).

69   Centers for Disease Control and Prevention. 2011. Gonorrhea - CDC Fact Sheet. Cdc.gov.   http://www.cdc.gov/std/gonorrhea/stdfact-gonorrhea.htm.   (Accessed June 2011).

70   Vanessa Cullins, MD. (updated 2011). Chlamydia. Plannedparenthood.org. http://www.plannedparenthood.org/health-topics/stds-hiv-safer-sex/chlamydia-4266.htm. (Accessed June 2011).

71   Vanessa Cullins, MD. (updated 2011). Pelvic Inflammatory Disease (PID). Plannedparenthood.org.   http://www.plannedparenthood.org/health-topics/stds-hiv-safer-sex/pelvic-inflammatory-disease-pid-4278.htm. (Accessed June 2011).

72   Tracee Cornforth. 2011. Urinary Tract Infections – UTI. About.com Women's Health. http://womenshealth.about.com/cs/bladderhealth/a/UTI.htm. (Accessed July 2011).

73   HerpesClinic.com.   Genital   Herpes   Statistics.   http://www.herpesclinic.com/ genitalherpes/genitalherpesstatistics.htm. (Accessed August 2011).

74   Centers for Disease Control and Prevention. 2011. The ABCs of Viral Hepatitis. Cdc.gov. http://www.cdc.gov/nchhstp/newsroom/docs/ABCs-of-Viral-Hepatitis.pdf. (Accessed August 2011).

75   Centers for Disease… The ABCs of Viral Hepatitis. Centers for Disease Control and Prevention. 2011. The ABCs of Viral Hepatitis. Cdc.gov. http://www.cdc.gov/ nchhstp/newsroom/docs/ABCs-of-Viral-Hepatitis.pdf. (Accessed August 2011).

Chapter 28: HIV/AIDS 101

76   Kaiser Family Foundation. 2005. U.S. Teen Sexual Activity. Kff.org. http://www. kff.org/youthhivstds/upload/U-S-Teen-Sexual-Activity-Fact-Sheet.pdf. (Accessed January 2011).

77   Centers for Disease Control and Prevention. 2002. Centers for Disease Control and Prevention. *Condoms and Their Use in Preventing HIV Infection and Other STDs*. cdc.gov. (Accessed September 2011).

78   "SIF#203-HIV 101." Hosted by HIV/AIDS Educator, Gay Rick. Sex Is Fun. Sexisfun. net. http://sexisfun.net/podcast/2009/12/2009-12-07-hiv.html. December 7, 2009.

79   Merck and Co. Inc. 2011. HEPATITIS B VACCINE (RECOMBINANT). Merck.com. http://www.merck.com/product/usa/pi_circulars/r/recombivax_hb/recombivax_ pi.pdf (Accessed July 2011).

80   Harvey Simon, MD, Editor-in-Chief, Associate Professor of Medicine, Harvard Medical School. 2011. Hepatitis B. nytimes.com. http://health.nytimes.com/health/ guides/disease/rubella/hepatitis-b.html. (Accessed September 2011).

81   HEPATITIS B FOUNDATION. 2005. Hepatitis B Foundation Participates in U.S. Capitol Briefing. http://www.hepb.org/pdf/Capitol_Briefing7_05.pdf. (Accessed July, 2011).

82   Gardasil.com 2011. INFORMATION ABOUT *GARDASIL. gardasil.com. http:// www.gardasil.com (Accessed August 2011).*

83   The Huffington Post. 2011. Study: Half Of Men May Be Infected With HPV. Huffingtonpost.com. http://www.huffingtonpost.com/2011/02/28/half-men-infected-hpv_n_829449.html. (Accessed March 2011).

84   Brian Alexander. 2011. Guys, Man Up and Get Vaccinated: HPV Is Your Responsibility.   MSNBC.msn.com.   http://www.msnbc.msn.com/id/41853611/ns/health-sexual_health/t/guys-man-get-vaccinated-hpv-your-responsibility/#. TmMd93PXExo. (Accessed March 2011).

Chapter 31: CONTRACEPTIVE/ SAFER SEX METHODS

85   Klickitat County Public Health. 2006. Abstinence. Kilckitatcounty.org. http://www. klickitatcounty.org/health/Content.asp?fC=168&fD=45. (Accessed February 2011).

86   Planned Parenthood (adapted from World Health Organization 2007). Comparing effectiveness of birth control methods. Plannedparenthood.org. http://www. plannedparenthood.org/health-topics/birth-control/birth-control-effectiveness-chart-22710.htm. (Accessed December 2010).

87   Ibid

88   Ibid

89   Ibid

90   Ibid

91   Ibid

92   Ibid

93   Ibid

94   Ibid

95   Ibid

96   Ibid

97   Ibid

98   Ibid

99   Estronaut. A Forum for Women's Health. 1999. Plan B: The New Morning After Pill. Estronaut.com.http://www.estronaut.com/a/Plan_B_Morning_After_Emergecy_ Contraceptive.htm. (Accessed 2011).

100   Planned Parenthood. Comparing effectiveness of birth control methods Planned Parenthood (adapted from World Health Organization 2007). Comparing effectiveness of birth control methods. Plannedparenthood.org. http://www. plannedparenthood.org/health-topics/birth-control/birth-control-effectiveness- chart-22710.htm. (Accessed December 2010).

101   Ibid.

102   Kate Zernike. 2006. Use of Contraception Drops, Slowing Decline of Abortion Rate. New York Times.nytimes.com. http://www.nytimes.com/2006/05/05/health/05abort. html. (Accessed May 2011).

103   B.A. Robinson. 2008. Major U.S. laws concerning abortion. Religioustolerance. org. http://www.religioustolerance.org/abo_supr.htm. (Accessed January 2011).

104   Planned   Parenthood.   http://www.plannedparenthood.org/health-topics/birth- control/condom-10187.htm. Condom. Vanessa Cullins, MD, MPH, MBA. 2011

105   The Emergency Contraception Website. 2011. Risk of Pregnancy. Princeton.edu. http://ec.princeton.edu/questions/risk.html. (Accessed July 2011).

SECTION VII - SEXUAL HEALTH

Chapter 34: SELF-EXAMS

106   National Cancer Institute at the National Institutes of Health. 2005. Testicular Cancer: Questions and Answers. cancer.gov. http://www.cancer.gov/cancertopics/ factsheet/Sites-Types/testicular. (Accessed June 2011).

107   (adapted from) Testicular Cancer Resource Center. 2009. How to Do a Testicular Self Examination: tcrc.acor.org. http://tcrc.acor.org/tcexam.html. (Accessed may 2011).

108   Mayo Clinic. 2010. Male Breast Cancer. Mayoclinic.com. http://www.mayoclinic. com/health/male-breast-cancer/DS00661. (Accessed January 2011).

SECTION VIII - SEXUAL HARM

Chapter 37: ABUSE

109   Carla Van Dam. 2001. *Identifying child molesters.* New York: Haworth Maltreratment and Trauma Press, P.50.

110   Wendy Maltz. 2001. The sexual healing journey: a guide for survivors of sexual abuse. New York: Harper's Collins, P.30.

111   Joe Kort. 2008. Gay affirmative therapy for the straight clinician: the essential guide. New York: W. W. Norton and Company, P.48.

112   National Center for Missing and Exploited Children. 2009.Statistics. missingkids.com. http://www.missingkids.com/missingkids/servlet/ PageServlet?LanguageCountry=en_US&PageId=2810. (Accessed August 2011).

113   Howard Snyder, Table 1: Age Profile of the Victims of Sexual Assault, 1991 – 96. Sexual Assault of Young Children as Reported to Law Enforcement: Victim, Incident, and Offender Characteristics, U.S. Department of Justice, Bureau of Justice Statistics, July 2000.

114   Bill Friedrich Ph.D., ABPP. ATSA 2004 Conference.Presented at Albuquerque, New Mexico. ATSA, October 27, 2004.

115   Prevent Child Abuse America. 2011. Fact Sheet: Sexual Abuse of Boys. http:// member.preventchildabuse.org/site/DocServer/sexual_abuse_of_boys. pdf?docID=127. (Accessed August 2011).

Chapter 38: ASSAULT

116   Koss, Mary and Harvey, Mary. (1991). *The Rape Victim: Clinical and Community Interventions.* Newbury Park, CA: Sage Library of Social Research.

117   Association for the Treatment of Sexual Abusers. 1996. "Reducing Sexual Abuse through Treatment and Intervention with Abusers," Policy and Position Statement. Presented at Beaverton, OR. ATSA Novermber 13, 1996.

Chapter 39: PERSONAL SAFETY

118   Susan Weiss. 2008. The Department of Health and Human Services Office on Women's Health. Date Rape Drugs Fact Sheet. http://www.womenshealth.gov/ publications/our-publications/fact-sheet/date-rape-drugs.cfm. (Accessed August 2011).

119   Response: Harvard Undergraduate Confidential peer Counseling. Harvard.edu. Sexual Violence in the United States. Hcs.Harvard.edu. http://www.hcs.harvard. edu/~response/about.html (Accessed December 2010)

SECTION IX - ONLINE SAFETY

Chapter 40: EXPOSURE

120   *Jerry Ropelato*. 2006. Internet Pornography Statistics.Toptenreviews.com. http:// internet-filter-review.toptenreviews.com/internet-pornography-statistics.html. (Accessed August 2011).

121   Bev Betkowski, Express News Staff. 2007. Rural teen boys most likely to access pornography, study shows. University of Alberta. Uofaweb.ca. http://www.uofaweb. ualberta.ca/expressnews_template/article.cfm?id=8248. (Accessed May 2011).

122   My Internet Safety Coach. 2009. Online Safety Statistics. Myinternetsafetycoach. com. http://myinternetsafetycoach.com/?p=18. (Accessed December, 2010).

123   Top Ten Reviews Internet Pornography Statistics *Jerry Ropelato*. 2006. Internet Pornography Statistics.Toptenreviews.com. http://internet-filter-review. toptenreviews.com/internet-pornography-statistics.html. (Accessed August 2011).

Chapter 41: EXPLOITATION

124   Internet Crimes Against Children. 2001. Youth Internet Safety Survey. http://www. ojp.usdoj.gov/ovc/publications/bulletins/internet_2_2001/internet_2_01_6.html. (Accessed July 2011).

125   Gavin De Becker. 1997.*The Gift of Fear.*New York: Dell Publishing.

Chapter 42: CHAT

126   National Center for Missing and Exploited Children and The Master Teacher. 2003. Teen Safety on Info Highway. Safekids.com. http://www.safekids.com/teen-safety-on-info-highway/. (Accessed November 2011).

Chapter 44: SOCIAL NETWORKING

127   Sex Laws.org. 2011. Sexual Offenses: Federal Law 18 U.S.C. 1466A – Obscene Visual Representations Of The Sexual Abuse Of Children. Sexlaws.org. http://www.sexlaws.org/18usc_1466a. (Accessed December 2010).

SECTION X - FOR PARENTS

INTRODUCTION

128   Facts on American Teens' Sexual and Reproductive Health. Guttmacher Institute. http://www.guttmacher.org/pubs/FB-ATSRH.html#n25 (Accessed September 2008).

129   Kaiser Family Foundation. 2005. U.S. Teen Sexual Activity. Kff.org. http://www.kff.org/youthhivstds/upload/U-S-Teen-Sexual-Activity-Fact-Sheet.pdf. (Accessed January 2011).

130   Ibid.

131   Internet Crimes Against Children. 2001. Youth Internet Safety Survey. http://www.ojp.usdoj.gov/ovc/publications/bulletins/internet_2_2001/internet_2_01_6.html. (Accessed July 2011).

132   The National Campaign To Prevent Teen and Unplanned Pregnancy. 2008. Sex and Tech: Results From a Survey of Teens and Young Adults. Thenationalcampaign.org. http://www.thenationalcampaign.org/sextech/PDF/SexTech_Summary.pdf. (Accessed August 2011).

133   American National Standard Safe Practices for Motor Vehicle Operation, American Society of Safety Engineers, Des Plaines, IL, 2006

Chapter 45: THE STATISTICAL REALITY

134   Premarital Sex the Norm in America. WebMD   http://www.webmd.com/sex-relationships/news/20061220/premarital-sex-the-norm-in-america.   (Accessed March, 2011).

135   Public Health Reports, 2007 Jan-Feb;122(1):73-8.

136   The History of Federal Abstinence-Only Funding. Advocates For Youth. http://www. advocatesforyouth.org/publications/429?task=view. (Accessed July 2011).

137   Impacts of Four Title V, Section 510 Abstinence Education Programs. Mathematica Policy Research Inc.   http://www.mathematica-mpr.com/publications/pdfs/ impactabstinence.pdf. (Accessed April 2011).

138   Facts on American Teens' Sexual and Reproductive Health. Guttmacher Institute. http://www.guttmacher.org/pubs/FB-ATSRH.html#n25   (Accessed   September 2011).

139   Deceptive Practices of Limited Service Pregnancy Centers. Planned Parenthood   Washington.   http://legalvoice.org/focus/health/documents/ LimitedServicePregnancyCentersReport1.2011.pdf (Accessed August 2011).

140   "SIF#116-Sex Education in America." Hosted by Kidder Kaper. Sex Is Fun. Sexisfun.net.   http://sif101-200.sexisfun.net/search?updated-max=2008-04-29T13%3A17%3A00-07%3A00&max-results=150. 4/10/2008.

Chapter 46: THE "GAY" ISSUE

141   Carol Lee. February 10, 2002. Gay Teens Ignored by High School Sex Ed Classes. Women'senews.org.   http://www.womensenews.org/article.cfm/dyn/aid/811/ context/cover/ (Accessed October 2011).

142   Susan Donaldson James. UNITED STATES: "Study Reports Anal Sex on Rise Among Teens" ABC News (December 10, 2008).

143   Increase In Anal Intercourse Involving At-Risk Teens And Young Adults. Medical News Today. http://www.medicalnewstoday.com/releases/130181.php (Accessed 2011).

144   William Saletan. Posted Tuesday, Sept. 20, 2005. Ass Backwards: The media's silence about rampant anal sex. Slate.com.   http://www.slate.com/id/2126643/ (Accessed October 2011).

145   "Sexual Health Statistics for Teenagers and Young Adults in the United States". Kaiser Family Foundation.http://www.kff.org/womenshealth/upload/3040-03.pdf (Accessed September 2011).

146   "SIF#114/115-Abstinence-Only Sex Education." Hosted by Kidder Kaper. Sex Is Fun. Sexisfun.net. http://sif101-200.sexisfun.net/search?updated-max=2008-04-29T13%3A17%3A00-07%3A00&max-results=150. 4/10/2008

147   Guttmacher Institute   http://www.guttmacher.org/statecenter/spibs/spib_SEpdf. State Policies in brief: Sex and HIV Education. (Accessed August 2011).

148   Russell and Joyner. 2001. "Adolescent sexual orientation and suicide risk: evidence from a national study". *American Journal of Public Health* 91 (8): 1276 – 81.

149   Jeremy Hubbard. "It Gets Better Project." ABC NEWS. http://abcnews.go.com/WN/dan-savage-project-world-news-conversation/story?id=11764984. (September 30 2010).

Chapter 47: ABSTINENCE-ONLY VS. COMPREHENSIVE SEX EDUCATION

150   Mathematica Policy Reasearch Inc. 2008. "Impacts of Four Title V, Section 510 Abstinence Education Programs" http://www.mathematica-mpr.com/publications/pdfs/impactabstinence.pdf. (Accessed April 2011)

151   Pamela K. Kohler, R.N., M.P.H.a,c, Lisa E. Manhart, Ph.D.b,c, and William E. Lafferty, M.D.a 2008. Abstinence-Only and Comprehensive Sex Education and the Initiation of Sexual Activity and Teen Pregnancy. Journal of Adolescent Health: 42 (4), 344-351.

152   Brigid McKeon. 2006. Effective Sex Education. Advocates for Youth. http://www.advocatesforyouth.org/publications/450?task=view (Accessed October 2011).

About the Author

Working in the helping fields for the last twenty years, Jo Langford has worked with kindergarteners through high school and college age students in medical, psychiatric and group-care settings as well as with families in their homes. He has spent the last decade with a private practice, providing comprehensive sex education, coaching and individual and group treatment for teens and their families.

He knows firsthand, the damage that can come from misinformation, lack of communication and fear around sexuality, and now brings information, education and humor to help underagers increase their knowledge and self-confidence as a proactive defense against the unfortunate consequences that sometimes accompany sexual activity.

Jo is a parent, therapist and sex educator in Seattle, Washington.

Made in the USA
San Bernardino, CA
20 November 2015